GCSE WORLD HISTORY

GCSE WORLD HISTORY

Ed Rayner and Ron Stapley

Longman

LONGMAN COURSEWORK GUIDES

COURSEWORK

Longman Group UK Limited,
Longman House, Burnt Mill, Harlow,
Essex CM20 2JE, England
and Associated Companies throughout the world.

© Longman Group UK Limited 1989
All rights reserved; no part of this publication
may be reproduced, stored in a retrieval system,
or transmitted in any form or by any means, electronic,
mechanical, photocopying, recording, or otherwise,
without the prior written permission of the Publishers.

First published 1989

British Library Cataloguing in Publication Data

Rayner, E.G. (Edgar Geoffrey), *1927–*
   World history – (GCSE coursework guides).
   1. England. Secondary schools. Curriculum subjects: History.
   GCSE examinations.
   I. Title   II. Stapley, R.F. (Ronald Frank), *1927–*   III. Series
   907'.6

ISBN 0–582–03864–2

Produced by The Pen and Ink Book Company,
Huntingdon, Cambridgeshire

Set in 10/11pt Century Old Style

Printed and bound in Great Britain by
William Clowes Limited, Beccles and London

EDITORS' PREFACE

The introduction of GCSE created many challenges for both teachers and pupils, not least the idea that, for most subjects, the grade awarded should be based not only on examination performance but also on the assessment of certain pieces of coursework. Whilst this concept has been welcomed in most educational circles as relieving some or all of the stress associated with examinations, it is also recognised as imposing other sorts of pressures on pupils. To achieve good results, it is necessary to keep up to date, be organised, and most importantly, maintain an appropriate standard *from the beginning of the course*.

Longman Coursework Guides have been written by experienced examiners to give GCSE candidates help with such tasks as choosing, researching and writing up topics. In addition, the authors give many examples of (and comments upon) typical student assignments.

We believe that the books will stimulate as well as instruct, and will enable students to produce coursework which will truly reflect the level of commitment and effort which the GCSE demands.

Geoff Black and Stuart Wall

ACKNOWLEDGEMENTS

We are grateful to the following for permission to reproduce material;

The Estate of David Low, for cartoons by David Low; The Guardian Newspaper for the cartoon by Gibbard on page 39; The Observer for the cartoon by Abu on page 51; The Sunday Express for the cartoon by Cummings on page 51; Punch Magazine for the cartoon by Mansbridge on page 73.

The illustrations on pp 28 and 29 are based on maps which first appeared in *A Sketchmap History of the Modern World* by Brian Catchpole (Heinemann 1974). The maps on pages 30 and 32 are based on illustrations which first appeared in *The Cold War* by Hugh Higgins (Heinemann, 1984).

CONTENTS

Editors' Preface
Acknowledgements

CHAPTER 1 Coursework in GCSE History ... 1
  UNIT 1 THE ROLE OF COURSEWORK IN HISTORY ... 1
    1.1 Summary of coursework requirements ... 2
  UNIT 2 SKILLS TO BE TESTED BY COURSEWORK ... 2
    2.1 Recall ... 2
    2.2 Cause and consequence ... 3
    2.3 Empathy ... 3
    2.4 Sources ... 5
  UNIT 3 COURSEWORK REQUIREMENTS OF EACH EXAMINATION GROUP ... 8
    3.1 London and East Anglian Group ... 8
    3.2 Midland Examining Group ... 8
    3.3 Northern Examining Association ... 8
    3.4 Northern Ireland Schools Examination Council ... 9
    3.5 Southern Examining Group ... 9
    3.6 Welsh Joint Education Committee
  UNIT 4 ADDRESSES OF THE EXAMINATION GROUPS ... 10

CHAPTER 2 Researching a topic ... 11
  UNIT 1 CHOOSING A TOPIC AND A TITLE ... 11
    1.1 Types of assignment ... 11
  UNIT 2 SOURCES OF INFORMATION ... 17
    2.1 Libraries ... 17
    2.2 Archive sources ... 19
    2.3 Museums ... 20
    2.4 Historical fieldwork ... 21
    2.5 History games and computer programs ... 21
  UNIT 3 METHODS OF INVESTIGATION ... 23
    3.1 Knowledge-based topics ... 23
    3.2 Documentary assignments ... 24

CHAPTER 3 Making the best use of visual material ... 27
  UNIT 1 MAPS, PHOTOGRAPHS AND CARTOONS ... 27
    1.1 Maps ... 27
    1.2 Photographs ... 33
    1.3 Cartoons ... 35
  UNIT 2 STATISTICS, GRAPHS AND DIAGRAMS ... 40
    2.1 Statistics ... 40
    2.2 Graphs and diagrams ... 42

CHAPTER 4 Preparing and writing coursework assignments ... 45
  UNIT 1 PRESENTING AN ASSIGNMENT ... 45
    1.1 Planning ... 45
    1.2 Preparation ... 46
    1.3 Completing the writing ... 48
    1.4 Examiner's mark scheme ... 50

UNIT 2	**PRESENTING A SECOND ASSIGNMENT**	50
	2.1 Planning and preparation	52
	2.2 Completing the writing	53
	2.3 Examiner's mark scheme	55
	2.4 Sources	56

CHAPTER 5 Examples of students' coursework — 57

UNIT 1 EUROPEAN UNITY — 57
- 1.1 Student's answer — 57
- 1.2 Examiner's comments — 58

UNIT 2 CHINESE AND CUBAN REVOLUTIONS — 58
- 2.1 Student's answer — 58
- 2.2 Examiner's comments — 59

UNIT 3 INDIA — 60
- 3.1 Student's answer — 60
- 3.2 Examiner's comments — 61

UNIT 4 STRESEMANN — 61
- 4.1 Student's answer — 61
- 4.2 Examiner's comments — 61

UNIT 5 MUSSOLINI — 62
- 5.1 Student's answer — 62
- 5.2 Examiner's comments — 64

UNIT 6 UN TROOP INVOLVEMENT — 64
- 6.1 Student's answer — 64
- 6.2 Examiner's comments — 67

UNIT 7 THE SECOND WORLD WAR — 68
- 7.1 Student's answer – version 1 — 68
- 7.2 Student's answer – version 2 — 69
- 7.3 Examiner's comments — 70

UNIT 8 ABYSSINIA — 70
- 8.1 Student's answer – version 1 — 71
- 8.2 Student's answer – version 2 — 71
- 8.3 Examiner's comments — 72

UNIT 9 VIETNAM — 73
- 9.1 Student's answer — 74
- 9.2 Examiner's comments — 75

UNIT 10 CHINA — 75
- 10.1 Student's answer — 77
- 10.2 Examiner's comments — 78

UNIT 11 MUNICH — 78
- 11.1 Student's answer — 80
- 11.2 Examiner's comments — 83

UNIT 12 THE POPULATION EXPLOSION — 84
- 12.1 Student's answer — 85
- 12.2 Examiner's comments — 87

UNIT 13 PLANNING THE PROJECT — 87

COURSEWORK IN GCSE HISTORY

> **UNIT 1** THE ROLE OF COURSEWORK IN HISTORY

So you have chosen History as one of your options for the GCSE. Good. We are sure that you have made a sensible choice, and although it is going to require a lot of hard work you ought to get considerable satisfaction and enjoyment from it. As with other subjects at GCSE you will be required to submit *coursework* as part of the examination. You will be tackling written assignments from the beginning of your course in the fourth year, so work from very early in the course may count towards your final assessment and grade. It is the aim of this book to help you get started in History coursework and to give you advice and guidance on how to do it well.

Each of the six GCSE Groups require coursework for all their mainstream syllabuses. If you are studying at a school, your teacher will have selected the Group and the syllabus for you. Depending on the Group, coursework in any of the Modern History syllabuses counts for between 20% and 30% of the final mark. It is therefore of considerable importance in determining your final grade.

> **Coursework is to your advantage**

The inclusion of coursework is intended for *your* benefit. In the previous exam system everything hinged on a two and a half hour examination at the end of the course. This placed a heavy dependence on luck and how you felt on the day. A student may have worked well throughout the two year course and yet the questions may not have suited him or her, so that the resulting grade proved disappointing. A heavy cold or the after-effects of the flu may have affected performance on the examination day. Of course, in GCSE the examination has not been abandoned: in fact there are usually two examination papers, whereas before there was often only one. With two papers the chances of having an 'off' day for *both* of them are less likely than with only one. But a substantial *coursework* element has enabled credit to be given for good work *throughout the year*. It allows students to work at their own pace, and it enables students to demonstrate historical skills without having to struggle to recall the evidence upon which to practise those skills, because they will have books and sources ready to hand. So it reduces the emphasis on speed and memory, and gives you the opportunity of gaining credit for the best work you have produced during the course.

There are various ways of *presenting* History coursework. There is nothing to prevent you submitting a tape, making a video, making a reconstruction model, recording an archaeological dig, or using artistic skills to present historical data in visual form. But the vast majority of coursework exercises will take the form of *written work*, even if this work is *supported* by drawings, photographs or sound recordings.

Many students (and parents) have the idea that coursework means the production of a detailed project which has involved vast research lasting many months, and which will approach book-size in its final form. The prospect of such marathon tasks across the range of subjects would be quite frightening if this were true. But happily this is not the case. It is the aim of coursework in all subjects to ask for something that is *manageable* and which arises directly out of the course itself. Nevertheless, in History it *is* possible that you will be asked for a *project*: the Midland Examining Group will allow you to present *one* piece of written work of up to 4,500 words. However, they do allow you to write as little as 2,000 words, and even these could be split into two pieces of work. These need only then be of *essay length*. The Welsh Joint Education Committee asks for an *extended essay* of up to 1500 words and three *short written exercises* arising out of class work. The Southern Examining Group asks for two *essays*, neither to exceed 1,000 words; the Northern Ireland Schools Examinations Council requires three *essays*, none to exceed 1,000 words; the Northern Examining Association expects from four to six *written assignments*, but these must not exceed a total of 6,000 words with a minimum of 3,000. It is generally true of all the Groups that work falling below the minimum number of words could well be penalised unless it is close to the required number, whereas work in excess of the maximum is unlikely to be penalised unless it exceeds the maximum substantially.

It is expected that much of the coursework required by *all* these Groups will consist of class essays, and that the best work will be submitted out of assignments regularly produced throughout the course. Naturally such assignments would have to cover the skills required, but your teacher will be aware of these when setting the assignments.

1.1 Summary of coursework requirements

More detailed information on each Group is given at the end of this chapter.

Group	Number of assignments	Length of assignments
LEAG	3	1,500 each maximum. 4,000 in total
MEG	1 or 2	2,000 – 4,500 in total
NEA	4 to 6	3,000 – 6,000 in total
NISEC	3	1,000 each, maximum
SEG	2	1,000 each, maximum
WJEC	4	1 at 1,500 – 3 much shorter

It has become the practice among the majority of Groups to require the submission of coursework proposals *in advance*. Thus the *titles* of the assignments, the basic *subject content* of the assignments, and some detail on *how marks will be awarded* have to be approved by the Group *before* any coursework is set or attempted. The aim here is to make sure that the assignments are suitable and meet the Group's requirements. It could be that a teacher, working in isolation, will otherwise set coursework which fails to test some or all of the required historical skills. To prevent this, the Groups ask teachers to submit their coursework proposals to the expert examiners and moderators employed by the Group. However, this makes it difficult for the candidate to devise his or her own coursework tasks. The Northern Examining Group is typical of those for whom advanced submission is compulsory, and it requires the notification of coursework details by 15 February of the *first* year of the two-year course. So you are likely to know specifically what is required of you in coursework by the end of your first term. If you want to submit your *own* coursework suggestions to your teacher, you will have to do so very early, and possibly within two or three months of starting the course.

UNIT 2 SKILLS TO BE TESTED BY COURSEWORK

The Groups specify quite closely *the skills to be tested* in coursework and the *proportions in which the marks are to be allocated* to the various skills. These proportions vary between the Groups. Most of them ask for *all four* major skills (see below) to be tested. However, the Southern Examining Group concentrates on the skill of seeing the past from the point of view of those who lived in it (empathy) and the skill of handling sources.

There are four abilities or *skills* that the coursework (and the examination) will be seeking to measure and test. These abilities are to be the *assessment objectives of the coursework part of the examination*.

2.1 Recall

Skill 1

The first assessment object is the ability 'to recall, evaluate and select knowledge relevant to the context, to analyse and synthesize such knowledge, and to deploy it in a clear and coherent form'. One of the things this means is that you must have the material of History to hand in doing the work – obviously not a difficult requirement in coursework, since you can have the books around you. But it also means that you must present the relevant historical material effectively. Of course, the *recall* ability is clearly more appropriate to examinations than to coursework, but *evaluation* and *selection* abilities are very important in coursework. Indeed, the Midland Examining Group allocates 40% of the coursework marks for this assessment objective.

2.2 Cause and consequence

Skill 2

The second assessment objective is 'the ability to make use of and understand the concepts of cause and consequence, continuity and change, similarity and difference'. In other words, students will be expected to show an understanding of *why* events happened and the important historical *consequences* of such events; they will need to be aware of *historical change* and the *pace* of change; and they will need to make historical *comparisons*, to point out historical *parallels* and to identify points of *similarity* and *difference*.

This ability will often be tested in *structured essays* (i.e. essays consisting of two or more parts or sections) which will be set in the *examination papers*. But some coursework assignments could be heavily weighted towards this assessment objective. An assignment which required a candidate to

> Use the given source material and secondary sources of your own choice to compare the effects of the Depression of the 1930s in (a) Sunderland and (b) Birmingham

would be testing partly assessment objective 1 for the *selection* and *arrangement* of material, and assessment objective 2 for the *comparison*, with similarities and differences being highlighted.

Such an assignment would obviously need suitable sources relating to the two towns which had been chosen by the teacher, but it may be possible for *you* to find some suitable documents yourself, and perhaps even to persuade your teacher to set a suitable piece of coursework based on them. Remember that in choosing your *own* documents for use in such cases, the danger is often that you will use too many documents rather than too few. A limited number of *relevant* documents that you can handle well will be much more use than a large number of documents of varying relevance which you handle badly.

2.3 Empathy

Skill 3

The third assessment objective is to look at events and issues *as the people in the past would have looked at them*. This means that students will be expected to judge events in the past and to comment on them from the point of view of those who lived at the time of the events. In order to 'look at events and issues from the perspective of people in the past' and to do it well, students will be expected to show that problems in the past were capable of being looked at in *different ways* by the people at the time. It is the skill of doing this that we call *empathy*.

There are broadly three levels of attainment in empathy:

▶ Those who recognise that people in the past had feelings and emotions, but mistakenly give to such people the ideas and feelings of the 1980s, will only have reached **Level 1** – and it is essential to get *beyond* this level in your coursework.

▶ **Level 2** is for those who correctly identify the feelings of people in the past *for that time period*, but then mistakenly assume that *everyone felt the same* at that time. It would be easy for students to suggest that in Hitler's Germany, for example, *everyone* wanted the Jews to be persecuted and *everyone* wanted a war as revenge for Germany's defeat in 1918.

▶ What is more difficult is to reach **Level 3** – to show that people thought *independently* and *differently* about the problems of their period – so that *some* Germans of the 1930s sympathised with the persecuted Jews for humanitarian or economic reasons, and *some* Germans feared a second World War or believed that it was wrong to seek for revenge.

Empathy work requires detailed *historical knowledge* to make it convincing and realistic. So the GCSE Groups are moving away from including empathy exercises in the written examination, and are now preferring to confine empathy to coursework, where it can score up to half of the marks (usually 30%) available for coursework. It therefore carries 15% of the total marks for the subject and it is very important to get it right. If you bear in mind, when tackling an empathy exercise, that you need to emphasise the *variety* of opinions held by people in the past, you will be on the right track. Of course, these opinions must be valid for the period. To suggest, for example, that the majority of Russians before 1914 opposed the Tsar because they were all good communists is factually inaccurate and, in terms of empathy, is firmly rooted in Level 1. But to demonstrate shades of opinion about the Tsar varying from hatred at one extreme to adoration at the other, and to use contemporary reasons to explain these shades of opinion, ought to get you to Level 3.

The sort of empathy exercise currently in use with the GCSE Groups specifically allows scope for showing various shades of opinion:

> It is September 1938. Hitler is asking for advice from Nazi leaders and generals on how to proceed in the dispute with Czechoslovakia over the Sudetenland. What sort of advice is he likely to have received?

Here it would be foolish to assume that Hitler would be offered similar advice from all those asked, and there is plenty of opportunity to reach Level 3. Some politicians might advise him to go ahead and put pressure on Czechoslovakia, assuming that Britain and France would do nothing and that without them the Soviet Union would be powerless to intervene. Others might point out the risk that if Czechoslovakia proved to be defiant to the point of war, Russia and France at least might well feel obliged to intervene. Here the generals might point to Germany's lack of preparedness, to the strong Czechoslovak frontier defences and the danger of being bogged down in a long drawn-out war. On the other hand, other generals might think it worth the risk and hope that Germany could win a quick, decisive victory by the use of superior air power.

Some questions may focus on one person, but they will be put in the form of a *problem* rather than in the form of role-play. You would not be asked, for example, 'As Lenin, explain why you made peace with Germany in 1918', but you might be asked

> In 1918 Lenin was considering whether or not to make peace with Germany and the other Central powers. Despite his call for 'Peace, bread and land' it was not an easy decision to take. Why was this?

Here you are not pretending to be Lenin, but you are expected to look at the problem of peace-making from Lenin's point of view. If you show why, despite Russia having an urgent need for peace, there were good reasons for some of those surrounding Lenin to urge him to break off the peace negotiations, then you are on your way to Level 3. To Lenin peace was essential, as Russia was no longer capable of effective resistance to the German armies. Lenin also needed peace to consolidate the Bolshevik revolution. Moreover, the Russian people desperately wanted peace; futile Russian offensives, enormously costly in terms of human lives, had caused mass desertions at the front, and the promise of peace had helped to make the Bolsheviks popular. But Lenin knew that German peace demands were outrageous: they were insisting on the Ukraine and the Baltic provinces as well as a large indemnity in gold. There was a danger that Bolshevik popularity would crumble away if such terms were accepted. Although Lenin consoled himself with the belief that the peace would be of short-term duration, because the Bolshevik revolution was about to spread worldwide (thus guaranteeing that Russia's sacrifices would be only temporary), there was the danger that reaction *against* the peace at home could kill off the Bolshevik revolution before it had a chance to spread into Germany.

The outlines given here for the German and Russian empathy questions are, of course, only *basic ideas* to help you reach Level 3. You would have to *develop* such ideas in depth in order to achieve the required length for your assignment – anything from 800 to 2,000 words. It is possible that you might be expected to write such assignments with the assistance of *secondary sources only*, i.e. history text-books and reference books, but this is unlikely. You are more likely to be given several pieces of *source material* – eyewitness accounts, letters, extracts from newspapers, photographs, cartoons etc. You will then be expected to build up your 'feel' for the period and the occasion by making effective use of them.

Sometimes the exercise will be a combination of an empathy exercise and a source exercise, in which case your work will be judged *both* for its empathy *and* for other skills in handling sources. If, however, you are provided with sources to use in an exercise which is testing empathy only, do *not* let yourself get sidetracked into an in-depth discussion and comparison of the sources and their validity.

It is, of course, possible that you may be given a role-play exercise. Don't panic! There are ways of dealing with this situation. Consider this task given to a student:

> As a victim of Stalin's purges who was lucky enough to survive, give an account of your experiences during the 1930s.

The student offered this answer:

> I joined the Party in 1917 and had taken part in the attack on the Winter Palace. As local party secretary I was bound to have heard rumours of arrests and disappearances, but I assumed that these were of non-party men who were plotting counter-revolution. Even when three workers at the munitions factory where I was employed failed to turn up for work, I saw nothing sinister in it. But at 3 a.m. next day there was a loud hammering at the door of the one-roomed flat I shared with my wife and two children, and I was hustled away to NKVD headquarters before I had time to dress. I was not physically ill-treated, but I was frequently wakened at night for interrogation. It seems that I had been denounced for anti-party activities, but as this was absurd I assumed that my release could

> not be long delayed. Here I was mistaken. My interrogators took the allegations seriously and they so wore me out with their questioning that I wondered after all if I had failed in some way, and whether perhaps I was guilty. I was not segregated from the other prisoners, one of whom gave me some nonsense of a warning that I should not say too much because informers had been planted among us. I considered this a tactic of police in capitalist states, and could only suppose that if it was true of our situation, and that was most unlikely, then some of the NKVD had become corrupt and Stalin should be informed of it.
>
> My interrogators told me that if I confessed I and my family would be treated leniently, and as they had now convinced me that I was guilty of anti-party activities, even if unintentionally, I decided to plead guilty. I was surprised to be put in the dock with fellow-accused whom I did not know, and charged with treasonable conspiracy. All of us, it appears had confessed, but one, Ivan, whose surname I cannot now remember, protested in court that his confession had been extracted from him by force. How low can a man get to save his skin? Anyway on the following day he repeated his confession and apologised to the court for his shameful behaviour. The man next to me whispered that Ivan had been drugged. It is amazing how these criminals let their imagination run away with them! Another muttered that the NKVD was in the pay of western capitalists, and that Stalin himself was in danger. What nonsense!! Anyway all were, myself excepted, sentenced to be shot. One told his judges that this was a poor reward after all he had done for Russia, but another said he would willingly die for the good of the Party. I was sentenced to twenty years in a labour camp, even though I had been promised lenient treatment, and I was a little hurt to hear myself described with the others as 'vile vermin'.
>
> Conditions in the labour camp were appalling. Food was of the poorest quality and meagre in quantity. The stove was inadequate to heat our hut during the long severe winters. Medical attention was generally non-existent, although the camp was plagued with epidemics and many died from disease or malnutrition. In our weakened state we were expected to do strenuous physical labour. Some clung to or turned to religion in order to survive, but as a true communist it would have been shameful of me to have followed their example. I was told in August 1941 that I was to be released, and despite the disbelief of many of my hut-mates, I am convinced that Stalin was kind enough to review my case personally. I was even lucky enough to get my old job back in the munitions factory.

This exercise is little more than 600 words long, and may be too short for some Groups' regulations. But it has quite a lot of empathy, despite its role-play format. Can you recognise it? The technique is to make sure that the hero of the role-play has *plenty of people in roughly similar circumstances with whom to disagree*, thus showing the wide variety of opinion required to reach Level 3. Our 'hero' disbelieves early stories of arrests, disbelieves rumours of informers, despises 'Ivan', is sceptical of drug rumours and rumours that the NKVD is in the hands of western capitalists, and shows the differing reactions of those sentenced to death. At the labour camp our 'hero' rejects religion, unlike many of his fellow-inmates, and does not share the scepticism of many of the other prisoners concerning the reasons for (and Stalin's part in) his own release. All these are pointers towards a good Level 3. If you are given such an exercise, you can tackle it in a similar way.

2.4 Sources

Skill 4

The fourth assessment objective is concerned with the handling of various kinds of *sources*. Some Groups, such as the SEG, devote half the coursework to this objective (as well as testing it in the examination itself) so it is very important to be familiar with all the various aspects of it. You will be expected to *distinguish between* primary and secondary sources.

Primary sources include photographs and artefacts (objects from the period), as well as written documents, all suggesting *first-hand* evidence (see below). We have already considered *secondary* sources, such as textbooks. You will also be expected to *understand* and *extract information from* the sources, to *interpret* the sources and to *distinguish between fact, opinion and judgment*. You should be able to *point out deficiencies* (gaps) in the material as evidence and any *inconsistencies* (usually where the evidence is contradictory). Particularly important, you *should be able to detect bias*. Finally you should be able to *compare* various types of historical sources and to reach *conclusions* based on this comparison.

Primary sources are first-hand evidence of history. A photograph taken at the time of a famous event, an object dug up from and contemporary with a famous battle, a cartoon published in a newspaper to comment on an event which has just occurred – all these are primary sources. So, too, is written or documentary evidence in which eye-witnesses are able to give an account of an historical event at which they were present (i.e. a first-hand account). Newspapers are contemporary with the events and issues they report, and although their evidence is not always first-hand, they are usually regarded as primary sources. Written sources which are compiled so long after the event they describe that they can no longer be thought of as contemporary are regarded as *secondary sources*. This is true of all history textbooks.

Of course, it does not follow that primary sources are necessarily *more reliable* than secondary ones. An eyewitness may see only part of an event; he may be biased, or he may have a particular viewpoint to justify. It is often easy to see this if two or more primary sources on the *same event* are compared. The killing of Jewish competitors in the Olympic games at Munich in 1972 was described in Jewish newspapers and many eyewitness accounts as 'murder by Arab terrorists'. But in much of the Arab world it was hailed as 'a blow struck for the Arab cause against Israel by brave Arab freedom-fighters'. The same kind of terrorist/freedom-fighter contrast can be seen in reports on events in Northern Ireland, as well as in the different ways the activities of the Afghan guerrilla fighters during the 1980s were reported in the Western and in the Eastern blocs.

The *conflict of view* in these events is obvious, and in such cases the *secondary* accounts of historians are likely to attempt a *more balanced* and less biased view. But it is important to remember that where you have only *one* primary source this may be just as one-sided as *Izvestia's* view of the Afghan rebels or the PLO account of the events at Munich. You may be unaware that your primary source has omitted or suppressed important evidence, but your approach to a *single unsupported source* should always take that possibility into account. Your task is, of course, easier if the source is using language which clearly *shows* its bias. Consider this description of Prime Minister Chamberlain on his return from Munich in 1938:

> Chamberlain looked a ridiculous figure in his outdated winged collar and ill-fitting suit. He appeared tired, and his monotonous voice showed relief rather than excitement. He waved in the air a piece of paper which looked about as flimsy as the promises written on it. Then he made his way straight to the House of Commons to boast to MPs of his proud role in the murder of Czechoslovakia.

Here Chamberlain is belittled by ridicule in the first line, and the word *monotonous* is intended in the second line to apply by extension to Chamberlain generally, rather than merely to his voice. Next the agreement brought back from Munich is belittled for its flimsiness, and the final sentence resorts to sarcasm on Chamberlain's responsibility for what happened to Czechoslovakia. This sort of passage lacks subtlety and is more likely to win sympathy for Chamberlain than condemnation.

Similarly some sources are immediately suspect because *political jargon* betrays their origin. Take this passage on the outbreak of the Korean War:

> The Imperialist warmongers of the West, alarmed at the economic success of the North Koreans, proposed rigged elections so that the South could take over the North. This suggestion was firmly resisted, and when liberation forces from the North moved into the South in response to the fraternal requests of the working-class of the South, the USA cynically manipulated the United Nations into agreeing to an illegal American invasion of Korea under the pretence of defending the South against communism, but in fact to prop up the corrupt Fascist regime of Syngman Rhee. The American intervention has held back the creation of a united socialist Korea, consigned millions of South Koreans to conditions of near-slavery, and has even threatened the living standards of the socialist miracle in the North.

While it may be argued that the standard Western account of the origin of the Korean War may itself be suspect, it is clear that this anti-Western account is even more extremist. Here there is *no attempt* to give a balanced account: its pro-communist bias is obvious. Some of the statements made are suspect (were there any 'fraternal requests', and has there been a 'socialist miracle in the North'?). The phrase 'Imperialist warmongers' loses its force through constant repetition in this and similar sources, so that it becomes mere communist jargon.

This sort of source should be easy to recognise. Remember though that the bias of a source does *not* make it valueless: it could be useful in demonstrating one contemporary viewpoint, and it may contain accurate, if selective, evidence; for example, the reference to Syngman Rhee would be difficult to challenge.

You might like to try another example:

> Let us see how far the promises of the government at the last General Election have been fulfilled. We were promised an economic miracle. Well it is nothing short of miraculous to have been able to achieve so many things in so short a space of time: to have trebled the number of unemployed, to have drastically reduced the purchasing power of the pound, to have virtually brought our housing programme to a halt and to have angered our trading partners in Europe and America: this is a record rarely before equalled. Only another term of office for the government could see this record broken.

It should not be too difficult to realise that the writer is hostile to the government, and that his reference to the 'economic miracle' is sarcastic. Readers are expected to conclude for themselves that re-election of the government would lead to more disasters of the kind here mockingly called 'miraculous'. Note that in this example it is not necessary to know whether the government in question is Conservative or Labour. If the text had made that clear, your own political sympathies might have clouded your judgment.

Sources which are *biased* may be unreliable for someone seeking the truth about what happened. But they may still be very useful to historians in showing the prejudices of their period or of their country of origin. Remember, too, that an apparently unbiased source may be defective. Compare the following:

> Several civilians were killed today, when government forces opened fire in the main square of the capital. Protests against the government's alleged brutality have been voiced in the United Nations General Assembly, and a Security Council resolution would be likely except that it would almost certainly be vetoed by Russia.

This seems very factual, it makes no attempt to provide a judgment and uses the word 'alleged' in dealing with the UN involvement, but United Nations disapproval seems to suggest that the government action must have been unwarranted. However, an account of the same incident in a second source gives a very different impression:

> A large crowd of demonstrators, after looting shops on the way, headed for the main square. Unable to break through the troops guarding the main public buildings the demonstrators began tearing up railings and paving stones and hurling these at the soldiers. After twenty minutes of this barrage, and when several soldiers were lying on the ground seriously injured, the order was given to disperse the crowd and a number were killed or injured in the firing that followed. The United Nations has called for a full report on the incident, and in the meantime Russia is blocking any moves to condemn anyone for what occurred until the report is published.

Perhaps you now feel that the first source is more biased than it looked at first. It omits the violence of the demonstrators, and it does not mention the UN investigation. It makes it clear that the troops acted under some degree of provocation (even if you think opening fire was too drastic), and the Russian attitude appears in a very different light if Russia is only trying to prevent the UN from jumping to hasty conclusions.

You may well ask which of these sources is to be preferred. They could *both* be deliberately misleading. With nothing else to go on, and no independent third source with which to make a comparison, you might cautiously prefer the source with the *greater detail*. The *omissions* in the first source have given a distorted picture, but it does not follow that the second source is any more reliable or accurate. Note the reference to an *independent* third source. If five sources give one account which is contradicted by two other sources, it may be tempting to accept the view offered in the five sources. But remember it could be that the five are all derived from the *same* original source and that the other two are independent of each other, and therefore more reliable. You may have no means of *proving* the common origin of the five sources, but at least in your discussion of the sources you could mention the possibility, especially if the suspect sources are very similar in detail.

Extended examples of the use of sources in coursework are given in Chapters 3 and 4. You should study these, and the shorter examples already given, in order to try to develop the right techniques and skills. The *extraction of information from sources* is an essential skill, but not a skill at a high level. If you are to achieve a high assessment from your teacher and the Examination Group you will need to *compare sources*, both for what they contain and for what they omit, and to *discuss the bias, reliability and usefulness of sources*. Before looking in Chapter 2 at how to set about choosing and researching a topic for coursework, it would be best to consider the requirements of the Examination Groups in a little more detail.

UNIT 3 — COURSEWORK REQUIREMENTS OF EACH EXAMINATION GROUP

3.1 London and East Anglian Group

> Look up the requirements of *your* group

This group will test assessment objectives 2, 3 and 4 in its coursework. Coursework will account for 30% of the total marks. Three pieces of work will be required, one for each of the three assessment objectives tested. The maximum for any one assignment will be 1,500 words with a normal maximum of 4,000 where all the assignments are written. Each of Syllabuses A, B and C has precisely the same coursework requirements. The assessment levels which the teacher should look for in marking the coursework are spelled out in detail for each of the various aspects of the three assessment objectives.

The following example lists the assessment levels for one aspect of assessment objective 2:

A study of continuity and change.

Target: *The ability to describe and explain the factors involved in a changing historical situation and those factors which remain constant.*

Level One: Gives a factual account of a situation or a series of events, the elements of change and continuity identified only implicitly.

Level Two: Explains factors making for change and continuity.

Level Three: Makes some links between factors and compares with past or explains rate or nature of change.

Level Four: Emphasises important factors, gives clear exposition of links and makes reasoned distinctions between major and minor factors.

From this you can see that a simple narrative account (Level 1) will not get you very far. Even a list of reasons for change or lack of it (continuity) will get you only to Level 2. Some linking and comparing these reasons will get you into Level 3, but if you want to reach Level 4 the linking has to be clear and effective, and you have to make clear the relative importance of points you are discussing (e.g. 'Point A is more important than Point B because . . .')

3.2 Midland Examining Group

Coursework will account for 30% of the marks for the whole examination. Each candidate will produce one or two pieces of coursework within a total word limit of 2,000 to 4,500 words. The coursework may in fact be several pieces of work relating to a common theme in Modern World History. This approach might be useful as all four assessment objectives must be demonstrated in the coursework, and this may be difficult to achieve in one set piece, such as a traditional project. The objectives are assessed in the ratio 40:20:20:20. Note that assessment objective 1 which is concerned with the selection, arrangement and communication of content has double the marks of each of the other objectives.

The assessment levels, for instance, for objective 1 are as follows:

Recall, selection, arrangement and communication of relevant knowledge.

Level 1: Mark range 1–3; shows ability to select and use some relevant information to construct answers/narratives/descriptions which are straightforward and accurate but are likely to be relatively brief or limited in scope.

Level 2: Mark range 4–7; shows ability to select and use a wider range of relevant information in the construction of answers/narratives/descriptions which are accurate and reasonably thorough but are nonetheless limited to the more obvious aspects of the matter under consideration.

Level 3: Mark range 8–10; shows ability to construct clear and detailed answers/narratives/ descriptions based on thorough and accurate use of a wide range of factual material. Shows appreciation of wider context of information used.

Here the difference in levels seems self-explanatory, but note that the marks are given out of 10. They would have to be scaled up and given out of 20 if there were two pieces of work or out of 40 if there was only one.

3.3 Northern Examining Association

At least four pieces of coursework are required. Between them they must test all four of the coursework objectives. To gain high marks these four pieces should reach a total of 3,000 words; more than 6,000 words will not normally be expected. Coursework counts for 30% of the marks for the whole examination. The assessment objectives are the same as those of the other Groups, and the levels of achievement are similar.

3.4 Northern Ireland Schools Examination Council

Coursework counts for 20% of the total marks for the examination. Three assignments are required, covering all the assessment objectives, and all three will be based on local studies. The first assignment of 750–1,000 words requires candidates to undertake a historical enquiry and to present it clearly and coherently. They will be expected to place their study in a wider historical context. Thus for example the Belfast Blitz should be seen in the context of the Second World War. This assignment also requires candidates to show skill in handling evidence, and this aspect will carry one-third of the marks. The second assignment is primarily concerned with cause, consequence and continuity. It also requires candidates to undertake a study of the reliability of evidence, and this element will carry one-third of the marks. This assignment should be 500–700 words in length. The third assignment is empathetic, designed to get candidates to 'show an ability to look at events and issues from the perspectives of people in the past'. This third assignment should also be 500–700 words in length. One third of the marks here will be for the effective use of evidence in contributing to empathy.

3.5 Southern Examining Group

The Group requires two pieces of coursework, neither to exceed 1,000 words in length. One must be concerned with assessment objective 3 (empathy) and the other is concerned with assessment objective 4 (the use of sources). Coursework carries 20% of the marks for the whole examination. The assessment levels for assessment objective 4 are as follows:

Level 1: Comprehension of the source.
Is able to extract relevant information from source; to extract specific related information from more than one source; to make simple inferences. *(1–3 marks)*

Level 2: Simple evaluation.
Is able to classify type of source; to comment on nature and tone of information provided; to detect omissions and bias; to distinguish between fact and opinion. *(4–6 marks)*

Level 3: Supported evaluation.
Is able to evaluate source by general sense of the period, in terms of author's situation or purpose, or by process of cross-referencing; use of source as evidence not as information; to draw reasoned historical conclusions. *(7–10 marks)*

The extraction of information from sources will score low marks (Level 1) unless it is backed by ability to classify sources as secondary and primary and to comment on the kind of source, the quality of its information and its probable reliability. Even this will reach only Level 2 and obtain less than 60% of the available marks. For Level 3 you will have to comment on the author's purpose in writing the source, see the source in its historical context, compare sources (cross-referencing), and see the sources as evidence rather than information. If you want to get the top marks you must see your sources in a wider historical context, and assess their effectiveness as evidence. Examples will be found in Chapters 4 and 5.

3.6 Welsh Joint Education Committee

Coursework carries 25% of the marks for the whole examination, and consists of an extended essay and three class exercises. Candidates will be required to write an extended essay on their chosen Modern World study theme, with a maximum length of 1,500 words. It must show candidates' ability to pursue independent research, to select and use relevant information, to understand historical concepts, particularly cause and consequence, and to record research findings in a clear and coherent form. To achieve these various aims, it will help if the essay is structured (i.e. sub-divided into several tasks). The following example of how this might be done is taken from the syllabus:

Superpower Rivalry
a) How far and for what reasons were the years 1960–62 years of tension and great rivalry between the USA and the Soviet Union?

b) Why and in what ways did the USA and the USSR develop a closer understanding or *détente* in the years that followed 1962?
c) What do you consider to be the main threats to peaceful relations between the superpowers today?

The extended essay carries 60% of the coursework marks. The other 40% are for 3 exercises undertaken in class. These are:

1 An evidential exercise based on at least two sources and requiring candidates to understand and assess sources. This is to be done under test conditions.
2 An empathetic exercise.
3 A past/present exercise in which candidates attempt to link past events with the current situation.

UNIT 4 ADDRESSES OF THE EXAMINATION GROUPS

As Groups revise their syllabuses from time to time it is important to obtain the *current syllabus* and to check carefully that there have been no recent changes or, if there have been, to make sure that you are fully aware of them.

You can ask your teacher for a copy of your syllabus. Alternatively you can write and ask for an order form to purchase your own copy of the syllabus. You will then have to complete the order form and enclose the cost of the syllabus and postage.

The names and addresses of the main Examination Groups are listed so that you can write and request an order form to purchase your own copy of the syllabus. You will then have to complete the order form and enclose the cost of the syllabus and postage.

London and East Anglian Group (LEAG)
The Lindens, Lexden Road, Colchester CO3 3RL
Tel: 0206 549595

Midland Examining Group (MEG)
Robins Wood House, Robins Wood Road, Aspley, Nottingham NG8 3NR
Tel: 0602 296021

Northern Examining Association (NEA)
31–33 Springfield Avenue, Harrogate, North Yorkshire HG1 2HW
Tel: 0423 66991

Northern Ireland Schools Examinations Council (NISEC)
42 Beechill Road, Belfast BT8 4RS
Tel: 0232 704666

Southern Examining Group (SEG)
Stag Hill House, Guildford GU2 5XJ
Tel: 0483 503123

Welsh Joint Education Committee (WJEC)
245 Western Avenue, Cardiff CF5 2YX
Tel: 0222 561231

RESEARCHING A TOPIC

UNIT 1 — CHOOSING A TOPIC AND A TITLE

“What kind of assignment is it?”

For the most part, you will find that your teacher will help you with your choice of assignment topic, and may well suggest a title. Indeed, the advance vetting of coursework assignments by the Groups may make *student selection* of coursework topics difficult and unlikely. Where there *is* room for you to have some say in the choice, you should be *guided by your teacher's advice*, since teachers are likely to have considerable experience of what is required, and to know what is possible within the limits of the average assignment.

The *nature of the topic chosen* should first be seen in relation to the *type of skills* which the assignment is intended to demonstrate. One that is intended to show your ability to handle a range of historical sources, to extract information from them, to compare them, to indicate gaps and inconsistencies in them, to detect bias, and so on, should be based on a number of pieces of evidence sufficiently substantial and numerous to be adequate for the task. You cannot, for example, make any kind of comparison between documents unless there are at least two of them.

“Look at the flowchart on p. 87”

An assignment that is intended as an *empathy* exercise should seek to avoid all the obvious pitfalls inherent in this kind of work. Choose a topic that demands *more than* role-play, and which does *not* limit you in your answer simply to *undifferentiated empathy*, as a newspaper obituary might do. Of course even an obituary *can* be written in such a way as to show *differentiated empathy* – by revealing, for example, that contemporaries have regarded the reputation of the deceased in different *ways*. However, this requires practice, and is not the easiest exercise to embark on at the beginning of the course. Avoiding this topic and choosing a more appropriate one for the purpose of showing *variety of opinion*, would be a good start for an assignment seeking to display skills of empathy.

An assignment intended to show your familiarity with *historical concepts* such as change and continuity, or similarity and difference, or one which demonstrates your *historical judgment* or your capacity to *evaluate*, should also be carefully chosen for this purpose. There is an example of this type of assignment in Chapter 1 (page 3).

The demands of the assignment should be clear from the title, and there should be sufficient scope within the title for these demands to be met.

1.1 Types of assignment

Examples of these three types of assignment – and there may be many others – will clarify and develop these points.

DOCUMENTARY ASSIGNMENTS

“Is it based on evidence extracts?”

If an exercise is based on *documents* chosen from the point of view of a possible *comparison*, the documents should clearly provide ample opportunity for a comparison to be made. Two such documents could be employed, for example, to illustrate the different attitudes towards the war in Vietnam held by the North Vietnamese leadership and the US government.

> We fight because North Vietnam has attacked South Vietnam . . . It is a war of unparalleled brutality . . . Small and helpless villages are ravaged by sneak attacks. Large-scale raids are conducted on towns . . . Over this war – and all Asia – is the deepening shadow of Communist China . . . The contest in Vietnam is part of a wider pattern of oppressive purposes . . . Since 1954 every American President has offered support to the people of South Vietnam . . . We must say in south-east Asia – as we did in Europe – 'Hitherto shalt thou come but no further.'
>
> *President Johnson, Address at Johns Hopkins University, April 1965*

> The Vietnam people have never done any harm to the US. But contrary to the pledges made by its representative at the 1954 Geneva Conference, the US Government has ceaselessly intervened in Vietnam; it has . . . intensified the war of aggression in South Vietnam with a view to prolonging the partition of Vietnam and turning South Vietnam into a neo-colony and a military base of the US . . . The US Government has committed war crimes, crimes against peace and against mankind. Half a million US troops have resorted to the most inhuman weapons . . . such as napalm, toxic chemicals and gases, to massacre our compatriots, destroy crops and raze villages to the ground . . . The Vietnamese people will never submit to force; they will never accept talks under the threat of bombs.
>
> *Ho Chi Minh to President Johnson, February 1967*

These extracts could provide material for questions depending on *factual information* or on *recall*, such as 'What were the arrangements agreed at the Geneva Conference of 1954?' or questions depending on the *understanding* of historical terminology, e.g. 'What is the meaning of the term "neo-colony"?' But obviously the documents offer the greatest scope for a *comparison* of the viewpoints of the two leaders, Lyndon Johnson and Ho Chi Minh, and this is how you could make best use of them.

Answers to questions involving a comparison of viewpoints must be *document-based*. It is not enough to make comparisons that are based solely on the *attributions* of the documents, and to say, for instance, that the first document is dated two years earlier than the second, that the first document originates from the President of the United States, whereas the second comes from the leader of the ruling group in North Vietnam. If you are not yet familiar with the word, 'attributions' means the labels attached to a particular passage to show where it came from, who said it, and when it originated. Effective comparisons must be based, not on these attributions, but on the *contents* of the documents themselves.

To a limited extent a comparison is a matter of *vocabulary*. The first document uses terms such as 'unparalleled brutality', 'deepening shadow' and 'oppressive purposes', all designed to produce unthinking support from the speaker's audience. The second document does the same with phrases such as 'the war of aggression', 'crimes against peace and against mankind' and 'the most inhuman weapons'. Such phrases reveal the *bias* of each speaker, i.e. his willingness to use, without discussion, the conclusions of political arguments he has not publicly examined, in order to achieve a 'knee-jerk' reaction of approval from amongst his supporters.

However, the comparison should largely be a matter of *content*. Both speakers present themselves in their most favourable light. The US President sees himself as the champion and the deliverer of oppressed native peoples, using phrases such as 'Hitherto shalt thou come . . .' which have almost a Biblical cadence, while Ho Chi Minh tries to command the higher moral ground by casting himself as the guardian of human rights against scientific barbarism by the uninvited intruders. There is a note of aggrieved innocence in his opening phrase – what did we ever do to *you*? The two documents, of course, give opposite sides of the picture. They cannot both be true simultaneously. Either the Communists are the oppressors and the Americans the deliverers, or the Americans are the oppressors and the Communists the deliverers. A good comparison will seek to explain and to illustrate the differences in their outlooks. To some extent it must presume a background knowledge of the Vietnamese War. You cannot, for example, begin to make any useful comparison unless you are aware who Ho Chi Minh actually *is*; your answer will be seriously weakened if you think he was the leader of the South Vietnamese and not the North Vietnamese. But this is not a context question, and does not involve the extended use of such background knowledge; to a large extent your answer will be built up from the material in the two documents themselves. In using this material you should not be afraid to employ selected quotations, if these illustrate your points well. This does not mean that you should copy out the passages in their entirety to avoid missing some shadow of meaning; the exercise is one of *selection* in picking out the most useful words and phrases.

This question involves a comparison between two very *similar pieces of historical evidence*: documents of much the same length and serving a comparable purpose. They are not in themselves substantial enough to form a complete assignment; more, or longer, extracts would be needed, with more questions, to fulfil this requirement. You can of course use more than just documentary extracts in your assignment. It would be possible, for instance, to compare two different *cartoons* dealing with a similar subject. It is also possible to compare together *different sorts of evidence*. A documentary passage could be compared with a cartoon – how far is the message of the one borne out by the other? A variety of other sorts of historical evidence (photographs, maps, graphs, statistics etc.) can also be employed.

It is unlikely that you yourself will be wholly responsible for choosing the evidence for this kind of exercise. But where you do have some influence, you should take care to choose the documents that are most appropriate for the exercise.

CHAPTER 2 CHOOSING A TOPIC AND A TITLE

EMPATHETIC ASSIGNMENTS

These provide you with an opportunity to demonstrate your ability to look at events and issues from the perspective of people in the past. This type of exercise is intended to combine two elements: your historical knowledge, and the acuteness of your historical perception. Such exercises are now less frequently tested in examination answers and more in coursework assignments, where the opportunities are greater for a convincing demonstration of empathy. Nevertheless, care should be taken with the *choice* of empathetic subjects, which may of themselves limit the possibilities.

> **Does it involve empathy?**

To illustrate this point, we shall consider some possible empathetic titles.

1. As a senior officer in the Nazi SS, prepare your speech of welcome to the new recruits into the Corps, indicating the importance of the basic concepts of Nazism to Germany in general, and explaining the special duties and responsibilities in the Nazi system of the SS in particular.
2. How would Sir Anthony Eden have sought to justify to his cabinet in the autumn of 1956 his decision to co-operate with the French in taking military action against Egypt?
3. A black American war veteran is to make a presentation to Martin Luther King in recognition of his services to the US civil rights movement. What comparisons would he make in his presentation speech between the conditions affecting American Blacks in the 1930s, '40s and the 1960s, and what successes in the civil rights campaign would he attribute to Martin Luther King's leadership?
4. Write an article for a British newspaper on the dismissal of Khrushchev, outlining the changes he had brought about in the Soviet Union during his period of office, and explaining his declining popularity there in 1964.
5. Explain the arguments (a) in favour of, and (b) against Britain's joining of the European Community in the first half of the 1970s. In the light of the present situation in Europe, do you believe the decision taken at that time was a wise one?
6. What arguments would have been used in the 1968 US presidential election campaign by supporters of (a) the Democratic candidate and (b) the Republican candidate, and how far did these arguments represent influences important at the time of the election?

Which of these titles *fails* to fulfil the primary requirements of an empathetic assignment, and for what reasons? Look again at number 5, and consider it from this point of view. There are two reasons for rejecting this title. In the first place, it is analytical and descriptive instead of being empathetic. It is perfectly possible to have memorised the arguments in favour of, and against, Britain's membership of the Community, without attempting to empathise with them. Furthermore, the second part of the question, demanding hindsight from the point of view of the contemporary scene, fails in the key requirement of 'looking at events and issues from the perspective of people in the past'. To choose this title might therefore present you with considerable difficulties.

Titles 1 and 3 both require you to put yourself in the place of someone in the past – the senior Nazi SS officer, or the black US citizen – and to see a particular situation in the way that person would have seen it at the time, speaking as he would have spoken and arguing in the way he would have argued. The weakness here does not lie in the nature of the subject-matter, though some people would argue that it is discreditable – even dangerous – to try to see history through the eyes of someone so blameworthy as an SS officer. (The same people would, however, probably approve of seeing things through the eyes of an underprivileged American negro, which shows how easily history can forfeit the impartiality it is so proud of possessing!) The real criticism of these titles is that they require you to impersonate an *imaginary historical person*, and speculate about the way such a character would have behaved. Such an exercise is said to be one of *role-play*, and is generally now believed to be a rather artificial and even fanciful one. Furthermore, it is a *one-dimensional* exercise, since it provides only an individual opinion, and conveys none of the diversity of contemporary opinion existing on any historical subject.

Title 2, requiring you to put yourself into Sir Anthony Eden's shoes, at least involves a *real historical person* instead of an imaginary one. But it shares some of the weaknesses of the earlier role-play exercises. In particular it is again *one-dimensional*, since it will offer the opinions only of a single individual, and can provide little indication of the different opinions which existed at the time of the Suez invasion. Indeed, the pitfalls of such an answer may be even greater; no-one can say with certainty that you are wrong in the way you interpret the thinking of an *imaginary* person, but the problem about impersonating a *real* person, and an eminent one, is that you may easily be accused of *misrepresenting* him. There is also the further pitfall in this case (which you could easily overlook) that the sort of arguments which might have been used in Cabinet may bear only a limited resemblance to those designed for wider public consumption.

Title 4 is also about a *real historical character*, but at least it concerns him at *second-hand* and not at first-hand, since it is about how an imaginary newspaper reporter would have written about Khrushchev. Part of the weakness here is that it is perfectly possible to give a *factual* account of the changes he brought about in the Soviet Union in the years 1953–64 without any *empathetic* interpretation of his role. Another potential weakness is that the reasons for his unpopularity in 1964 are seen substantially in the same light at the present time as they were when Khrushchev was overthrown. There is therefore no *guarantee* that the answer you give to this question will be regarded as empathetic.

Answers to a title such as 4 above therefore have two possible faults: first, they represent the views of a single imaginary newspaper reporter, and are *one-dimensional*; and secondly, they are more *analytical* then empathetic. Nevertheless, it is worth observing that a good empathetic answer *could* be written in answer to this question, and of the five titles *examined so far*, this is probably the most effective. Part of such an article, for instance, could be written along the lines suggested below:

> . . . Opinions vary both in Britain and the Soviet Union on the significance of the changes Khrushchev introduced during his period of power. Khrushchev's relaxation of the Soviet police state appears to us to be bold and brave; but many would argue that it has not gone far enough and that firing squads have merely been replaced by psychiatric hospitals. His economic reforms, too, have commendably tried to encourage initiative, enterprise and efficiency, but have offended many of the party élite: we would welcome the significant improvement in the provision of consumer goods, but some would say his success is undermined by the disaster in the Virgin lands.

Development of this style of treatment shows *various viewpoints*, and if sustained would be classified as *differentiated empathy*.

Of all six titles, however, *number 6* is clearly the most appropriate for the purpose. Weak answers, of course, could still be written on this topic. A student might produce a *simple list* of the issues important at the time of the 1968 presidential election, without any empathetic grasp, and go on to state that *all* political arguments represent factors important at election times. But 'good' answers could very well be written on this topic. You could show an empathetic understanding of how strongly the issue of Vietnam figured in 1968, and how this foreign issue was linked to the many other vital domestic issues (urban decay, welfare reform, civil rights, etc.) that went along with it. The best answers might tackle matters other than the issues involved, and even suggest that the outcome of the election was more a matter of personality than it was of policies. Equally a good answer might examine the forces at work in the USA in the autumn of 1968 and the structure of American politics, and suggest that after eight years the country was ripe for a change of government. But whatever line they took, good empathetic answers would show an understanding of what America was like at the time of the 1968 presidential election. They would therefore fulfil the primary requirement of empathetic answers.

Though it is desirable that coursework assignments directed towards empathy should be very carefully selected, empathy need not of course be limited to questions that are specifically designed to test it. *Any* extended piece of historical writing, if it shows a mastery of its subject, will probably have significant empathetic overtones. A good piece of *biographical work*, for example on Colonel Nasser, will show a sensitive appreciation of his situation and his difficulties during the years he was in power in Egypt, and will endeavour to look at his problems in much the same way as Nasser looked at them himself. Again, good work on the Cold War will show some ability in appreciating the point of view *of both sides*, and will not – unlike newspaper accounts – identify exclusively with one partisan viewpoint or the other. In other words, empathy may show itself in any historical writing concerned with personalities, events and situations.

EVALUATION OR ASSESSMENT TOPICS

In this case, too, the choice of subject can be all-important. Again it may be useful to consider some possible titles.

1. British military strategy at the time of the launching of the Falklands War in 1982: how adequate was British planning?
2. How effectively did German economic controls operate under the Nazis before and during the Second World War, and how far can the breakdown of the German economy be held responsible for defeat in that war?
3. 'British policy in Palestine in the years 1918–48 was morally unjustified and contrary to the promises made to the Jewish community at the time of the Balfour Declaration.' Do you agree? Explain your answer carefully.

4   The women's history of twentieth-century western Europe.
5   Wartime evacuation: how far were the objectives of government policy achieved in practice during the Second World War?
6   A bid for power: what were the real political motives of Winston Churchill at the time of the General Strike in 1926?

Most of these titles attempt to examine *a particular historical problem*, in a way that is appropriate for an assignment of the length required. In choosing a topic, it is extremely important *not* to select a title that is purely narrative or descriptive, such as the following:

7   An outline of the war in Korea, 1950–53, with an account of the settlement at the end of the war.
8   What were the features presented by developing countries in the second half of the twentieth century?

> **Does it involve evaluation or assessment?**

Details of both these subjects may be found in secondary texts, so that by borrowing passages from carefully selected accounts you could produce respectable answers without much effort. This 'scissors-and-paste' method is frowned upon by GCSE assessors: it defeats the underlying motive of the assessment, which is to stimulate some (admittedly limited) research activity by candidates. Topics ought to cover something *more limited* and *more precise*. This enables you to explore more thoroughly a particular corner of history, and, rather than repeating what *others have already found*, to make your *own* contribution to the examination of the problem. Your title may even take the form of a question, in order to provide a sharper focus to the issue under consideration.

Nevertheless, considerable difficulties remain for an evaluation assignment, and it is helpful to be aware of them in advance. Examine the six titles suggested at the head of this section and see if you can work out what these difficulties are.

Title 1 refers to recent events, has been given extensive coverage and will probably yield good maps and illustrations which can be used or adapted for your work. The trouble arises from the use of the word 'adequate' in the second part of the title. Adequate for whom, or for what? The meaning here, pretty clearly, is 'for the purposes of the British military campaign'. However, the answer to the question is largely a matter of individual opinion, and in a problem of this kind you will probably find that even the experts are far from being in agreement. You could usefully examine the *extent* of their agreement or disagreement, by setting out the two sides of the controversy and so illuminating the fundamental issues, but unfortunately you might well find yourself in a position where you were not even able to do this. The fact is that much of the information relating to the Falklands War is *classified*, i.e. it is unavailable for examination because it is still secret. You could of course limit yourself to the newspaper coverage of the war, and thus avoid arousing the curiosity of MI5, but to do this would be rather like relying on the *Normandy Evening News* for coverage of the battle of Hastings!

Non-availability of evidence is also likely to be a major stumbling-block in the case of title 2. Insofar as the Nazis kept any consistent and reliable record of their attempts to control the economy, much of the available documentary evidence on this was destroyed during and after the Second World War. What is more, the evidence remaining is largely located in Germany and is written in the German language. Bearing in mind that such evidence would be difficult enough to interpret, even if it were complete and in English, you might be well-advised to think again before embarking on anything so ambitious.

'Moral justification', in title 3, makes the question impossible to answer. What appeared to be 'moral justification' to one person would be seen quite differently by another. In the same way, an observer who *approved* of British policies in Palestine during the years of the mandate would have no difficulty in showing that British actions were fully in line with the promises which Britain had previously made, while one who *disapproved* would have no difficulty in doing exactly the opposite. It is easy to see that widely different views would be taken by Jews and by Arabs, and there are probably wide differences even between the Jews themselves. To ask this question, therefore, is rather like asking 'How long is a piece of string?'

Title 4 opens up new problems. For one thing, its subject-matter is far too wide to be covered in an assignment of GCSE length. Although the topic is a fashionable one, its title is loose and rather indeterminate. 'Western Europe' is fairly precise, and 'twentieth-century Western Europe' is better still; but does 'The women's history' mean the history *of* women, or the history *for* women? If a history *for* women is intended, does this mean that their understanding of the subject is *different* from men's, and that the assignment must be written at a different level, as if, for example, it were 'A children's history'? And if it is a 'history *of* women', what is it likely to say? Will it say that men have had all the fun, but women have been given all the dull, repetitive tasks of domestic life? This may be quite true, and indeed worth saying. However, in this form it would be *social comment* rather than historical evaluation, with no link to recognisable historical events or trends. Perhaps the most important guideline in the choice of assignment topic has been overlooked: *it must be about history*.

The subject-matter of title 5, on the other hand, is *limited* and *distinctive enough* to be chosen as the topic of an assignment. It is not too difficult to find out what the objectives of the British government were at the time they ordered the evacuation of children from towns and cities threatened by the German *blitz* at the outbreak of war in 1939. This is covered in government circulars to local authorities and in other publications dating from that time; a lot of evidence is also provided in secondary texts. It is possible to find out a good deal about the experiences of the evacuees themselves, especially if you live in a place that either dispatched, or received, evacuees. You may have someone in your family or among your family friends who will give you a *first-hand account* of what it was like to have been an evacuee. If so, you might get very excited and record their comments on tape. But you should remember that your brief is *government policy* rather than the experiences of evacuees. You should remember too that the recollections of individuals can become dimmed and inaccurate with the passage of the years. Nevertheless you will find County Record Offices with useful contemporary material (written documents, letters, photographs, official information and so on) covering their part in the evacuation arrangements, and you will also be able to locate and to study collected biographical experiences, especially those written down at the time, or shortly afterwards. It is quite possible that you will make a worthwhile and interesting contribution, though a modest one, to historical research, and that others later, following your lead, will be able to do the same thing in their own localities.

The same is true of title 6. Though it is very unlikely that you will find local information to help you with this assignment, you will find useful secondary accounts and a good many published sources, especially personal memoirs. Personal memoirs relevant here might include those of Stanley Baldwin, Joynson-Hicks (the Home Secretary), John Reith of the BBC and even the Archbishop of Canterbury. All these have a bearing on the question of whether Churchill, in his vigorous campaign against the General Strike of 1926, was merely seeking to subdue the strikers, or whether he was aiming to oust Baldwin from his leadership of the Conservative cabinet and become Premier himself. This is a historical study which is not only worthwhile but also interesting, both to the student and to those who evaluate the finished work. The documents themselves do not deal specifically with this issue, but they provide you with enough information to *produce and evaluate a theory*, and therefore to make your own small contribution to historical knowledge.

Provided enough thought and care is devoted to choosing a good subject, both *national* and *local* themes can be dealt with in a history assignment without resorting to the mechanical methods of 'scissors-and-paste.'

Questions can only usefully be dealt with, of course, when the *evidence is available* to enable them to be answered. You may find that you have asked a question which simply cannot be answered. In cases such as this – and there may be quite a number – you have no choice but to *modify the question* until it *can* be answered. This process, especially if repeated, can move you some way from your original point of departure. You may even have to abandon your enquiry altogether, and seek another starting point.

Procedures for an evaluation/assessment assignment

A useful procedure, therefore, for such an assignment, i.e. one in which you have a choice of subject, would be as follows:

1. *Select* a general area of enquiry, and formulate a working question.
2. Amass your *research material*, using footnote references in one book to lead you to another. Amass archive references to the local County Record Office (CRO) where these are available and relevant.
3. *Modify* your working question in the light of the contents of your research findings. When you have arrived at a question which you believe *can* be effectively answered, settle on your final title.
4. Set out the steps by which the question can be answered as *separate sections* of your work, and rough out the intended contents of each of these sections.
5. Write a *draft* of each of these sections, and produce the first draft of your assignment. Satisfy yourself that you have adequately answered your question.
6. Write out your assignment in its *final form*, providing it with a title page, a table of contents, a bibliography, and an index, and inserting any illustrations, photographs etc. Remember that this is not a photograph album, and that your text should not be overloaded with illustrations. (The only exception to this would occur where the subject-matter of your assignment dealt specifically with the photographic coverage of a particular occurrence.)
7. Always work well within your *deadlines*, and set yourself intermediate deadlines for the stages mentioned above. This avoids rushing the final version of the work.

The selection and development of a subject should provide you with an enjoyable as well as a fruitful enterprise. At all stages you should *consult with your teacher* and take heed of any advice you are given, as outsiders may sometimes identify flaws or make suggestions that you would not necessarily have thought of for yourself. Remember too that it is your teacher who is going to assess the work and give a mark for it.

The stages outlined here relate to a *project*, which is a *major piece of coursework*, though they can be applied to other, shorter, pieces of work. It is not necessary for those who have to produce assignments of 800–1000 words (as for SEG) to produce an Index, but it might be desirable where the coursework consists of one major piece of writing. In the vast majority of cases your teacher will be setting the assignments and providing the sources, though there will still be some scope for individual students to seek out further material.

UNIT 2 SOURCES OF INFORMATION

In many cases students will find themselves provided with copies of historical source material by their teachers, or at least with some indication of where this material can be found. Nevertheless, it will be useful if you know a little about these sources on your own account. What follows is general guidance on the subject of the *location and use of historical source material*.

2.1 Libraries

❝ Use your library ❞

Most students will be able to use their *school or college library*, and have access to the material stored there. It is however important to join other libraries as well – which in most cases will mean the *local public library*. Though there may be a small joining fee, the services of these libraries are otherwise free.

When you are familiar with the layout of libraries you will see that they provide you with access to a good deal of valuable source material. They are chiefly organized into three sections:

▸ *borrowing facilities*, which enable you to remove books from the premises to study at your leisure (though with a stated limit on the period of borrowing);
▸ *reference facilities*, which enable you to consult books without removing them (though many reference departments have excellent reprographic machines which allow you to take photocopies of important pages to use for study purposes);
▸ *inter-library loans services*, which enable you to secure books not available in your library by borrowing them from other libraries.

You will find that libraries provide you with the following sources:

▸ Books
▸ Articles in handbooks, encyclopedias etc.
▸ Yearbooks
▸ Periodicals and newspapers

BOOKS

At first sight, the vast numbers of books in a public library may seem daunting, and first of all you must learn your way about. If you are unfamiliar with the layout of a library, especially if it is a large one, it will help to spend a little time walking round the shelves and getting to know the general location of the material. You will also soon learn that you are expected to be reasonably quiet, and to be considerate of the needs and interests of other library users.

For coursework purposes, you will find it is the non-fiction books in which you are interested. For convenience these are arranged in nearly all libraries into the *Dewey Classification*. Each book is given a classification number, which is displayed in most cases on its spine. The Dewey classification divides human knowledge into ten categories:

    000   General Works
    100   Philosophy
    200   Religion
    300   Social Sciences
    400   Languages
    500   Science
    600   Technology
    700   The Arts and Recreation
    800   Literature
    900   Geography, Biography and History

Each of these classes is sub-divided to specify subjects in greater detail. English history, for example, is classified as 942, and may be sub-divided further in accordance with period and subject matter e.g. 942.789. This numerical classification is often followed by the first three letters of the author's surname. In books which have a biographical dimension, the first three letters of the subject's name are often added, for example LLO for Lloyd George. Hence Lord Moran's biography of Winston Churchill has as its classification 942.829 CHU/MOR. This system means it is fairly easy to locate the books you need by checking the numbers.

To discover whether a library has the book you require you should learn to use the *card index*, or, in modern libraries, the *microfiche index*. Both of these record all the books the libraries hold in alphabetical order, both by author and by title. Using the index is the best way of finding out whether a library has a copy of a given book, since you can hunt along the shelves for a long time without finding it – or it may have been taken out by a previous borrower. There are other ways of tracing the existence of books, for example through the use of a cumulative book index, but these are more difficult, and will probably require you to ask the librarian on duty for help. Asking the librarian is often a good idea, and you will find librarians only too keen to help. Of course, you should try not to be vague.

Student: 'Have you any books on British History?'
Librarian: 'What period?'
Student: 'I'm not sure; I think the nineteenth century would do.'

This kind of request is unlikely to fire the imagination of the librarian, and may well induce irritation! The more specific you can be, the more likely it is that the librarian will find what you need.

Learning to find your way round a book is perhaps rather simpler. Most books have a *table of contents* in the front, and an *index* in the back to guide you to the places in the text where specific topics are covered. The index can also save you reading through a great deal of irrelevant material in search for a particular piece of information. Many books also have, either at the front or at the end, a *bibliography* of the books used, or recommended, by the author. Some books contain further bibliographical references tucked away in footnotes scattered through the text. Bibliographies and footnotes can often alert you to further sources of information which you might otherwise have missed.

You should always remember, when making use of a book, to *record* the appropriate particulars in order to be able to refer back to it later. In the notes you have taken, you should attach details of the *title*, the *author*, and the *publisher* of the book, the *Dewey classification* (where there is one), and the *pages* and *chapters* from which the notes came. There is nothing more annoying than taking notes from a book and not being able to refer back to it later because you have forgotten what it is. The same thing, incidentally, is true of archive and other sources: you should always note the index number in case you need it again at a later time.

If, after a thorough search, you finally discover that the library does not have a copy of a particular book that you need, then you could ask the inter-library loans service to obtain the book from the nearest library where it is held. Remember that although inter-library services are very good, there is always a time-lag. Getting a book from within the county area may take several days, but getting one from further afield may well take two or three weeks.

OTHER LIBRARY RESOURCES

Reference departments are organized in a similar way. However, you cannot borrow the books they hold, but must consult them on the spot. Reference departments will hold, in addition to books of the ordinary type, encyclopedias, dictionaries of biography (national and international), yearbooks, handbooks and the like. A number of them also keep periodicals on file, and possibly even daily newspapers.

Encyclopedias are probably the most important reference sources, since the best of these combine the functions of an atlas, a gazetteer, a dictionary, a who's who and a compendium of knowledge. Though they are not designed for the specialist, you will find they provide very useful information. Probably the best of the encyclopedias is the *Encyclopedia Britannica*, which went through 14 editions before the present editorial policy of continuous revision was introduced. You should refer to the front of the volume you are using to find out how old it is, so you can be sure that the information is fairly up-to-date. Other well-known encyclopedias include *Chamber's Encyclopedia*.

Dictionaries of dates are kept by a number of libraries, and may be useful in providing accurate information of this type. Reference books such as the Longman *Handbook of Modern British History* provide a great deal of material besides dates. There are student equivalents of publications like these, for instance the Longman *GCSE Factfinders* in History.

It is impossible to list all the other reference books which you may find useful, but you ought to be aware of the existence of:

- *Keesing's Contemporary Archives*, which gives a brief digest of world news at frequent intervals, all of which are collected and bound together by libraries to give a contemporary summary of developments. There are other, simpler, versions of this production which are targeted on students of school age.
- *Statesman's Yearbook*, published annually, which provides detailed information and statistics, mostly arranged geographically.
- *Whitaker's Almanack*, also published annually, provides similar information.
- *United Nations Yearbook*, which deals with the transactions in the UN. It has up-to-date statistical information (as far as this is available) on a large number of topics, though some of the information appears in an unusual format i.e. in English and in French on facing pages.

Newspapers are kept in some library reference departments, although often back copies of only one or two national papers such as the *Times* or the *Guardian* are kept. You may find, however, that back copies of local newspapers are on record, and these may well turn out to be useful in connection with a local assignment. Unfortunately, not all newspapers are equally reliable, and some, especially the local ones, do not always report events accurately. Hence, in using newspapers as sources, you should always be cautious in accepting their accounts. Many older newspapers are by this time in a fragile condition and should be handled very delicately for fear that they tear or crumble. For this reason, many libraries have put their newspapers on microfiche, and these are now read by means of a viewer (some with an inbuilt photocopying facility). If you wish to refer to a large number of newspapers, and you are fortunate enough to live in the London area, or are able to visit London, you could make a journey to the newspaper library at Colindale in North London, which has very extensive newspaper records.

Do not be afraid to ask for the guidance of the reference librarian if you need it; this can save a great deal of wasted time in a vain search for a book or periodical. Librarians are always willing to help with genuine enquiries, so long as you take care to make your enquiry as clear as possible.

2.2 Archive sources

Archive sources

Nearly all county towns have a *County Record Office*, or CRO, a local repository of archive material. A number of these have already established close relations with schools and colleges, and have packaged materials which may be useful in the preparation of coursework assignments. Students living in London are fortunate also to have near at hand a number of national archive sources such as the *Public Record Office*, or PRO, but it is less likely that GCSE students would wish to use this.

It is best to be introduced to your local CRO properly, either by arranging a visit with your teacher, or asking your teacher for a letter of introduction. Archivists do not appreciate students wandering aimlessly through the record office without any clear idea of what they are doing. Many CROs issue membership cards to their users, and require visitors to sign the visitors' book at every visit, partly as a security precaution. All of them operate on strict rules: no coats or bags in the searchroom; documents to be signed for when collected from the searchroom supervisor; pencils only to be used in the searchroom; damage to, or markings on, documents to be avoided, and so on. You should also make sure you know the times when the CRO will be open, particularly if you have to travel some distance in order to visit it.

You will find that all the documents or groups of documents in a CRO are carefully numbered and their particulars recorded in an extensive card index. This classifies them by subject matter and in other ways. There is little point in browsing through the index unless you have some idea of what you want. You should at least clarify your intentions to some extent before embarking on your trip. Your teacher or the archivist on duty will be able to give you a general idea of the strengths of the Office. This is the point from which you ought to begin, in order to find out what other material may be helpful.

When you have eventually located and used an archive source, you should carefully note its index number before returning it to the archivist. Put this in your notes along with the material you have noted from the source, so that you can easily refer to it again in the future if you need to.

You will find there are two main types of archive source which may be of value to you in your work: material with a national connection, and local material.

MATERIAL WITH A NATIONAL CONNECTION

Important national movements may have had an impact on your local area, and your CRO may have a good set of records showing this. You may for example find that the CRO is useful in offering material on the General Strike of 1926, or material referring to the part played by local people in the Blackshirt Movement of the 1930s, or the Campaign for Nuclear Disarmament in the 1950s. The evacuee theme referred to above on page 16, of course, is an example of a national matter which had local implications. At the same time, it does not follow that any of these themes *will* be fully documented, even in an area which should have been connected with these movements, since there is often a 'hit-or-miss' quality about local records. Conversely you may well be surprised to find that there are excellent records even on a topic where you would not really have expected it. These documents may then be studied in conjunction with contemporary press records. A useful project title here would be: 'How did such-and-such a national movement affect Cityville or Loamshire at such-and-such a time?'

LOCAL MATERIAL

Material that is purely of local importance may also be represented in the CRO. Sources to do with local experiences during the blitz, or the impact of rationing, or the construction of a motorway may be available, and there may be good collections of material in the form of personal letters or diaries. There may be information relating to the history of a particular school or college, its rebuilding or closure. You may find valuable sources of social history well represented: slum clearance and rehousing is one such subject, where records may show how a population has been moved from one area of the town to another, to live in quite different situations and in different types of property, and highlight the differences that this move produces in their way of life, as well as on the local maps. Other social themes may include changes in the employment pattern over the last fifty years, standards of living and living conditions before the war, the end of trams and trolley buses, local fairs or carnivals and so on. It is worth saying that what you will *not* find is material of fairly recent date. The records of when and how your school became a comprehensive school, for instance, will still be regarded as sufficiently sensitive not to have reached the public shelves; in the same way, matters relating to people who are still living will not be within your reach.

Suitable areas of study should be discussed with your teacher, who may well be able to link this primary archive material to secondary sources in the form of specialist books on housing, leisure habits and so on. If you have spent some time examining original source material, you should explain to your teacher exactly what information you have to hand, so that your teacher can get some idea of whether your suggestion will work. It may well be that from the particular angle you have been following, *you know more than your teacher does on the subject*.

Archive material should be used to help you *reach conclusions* in your project work, but it should not merely be reproduced or summarised. The mere act of locating archive material and copying it is not specially creditworthy. Giving a summary of the contents of the documents and reproducing the archive material in appendices does not add significantly to the sum of historical knowledge. It is your job to *interpret* the material, and to relate it to the theme that you are investigating. After all, other people can easily locate the archive documents themselves: if all you do is to reproduce what the documents *say*, you have not made any important use of them.

You should bear in mind that the writers of general secondary texts may well be unfamiliar with the primary documentary material that you may find in archive sources such as CROs. To be able to bear out, or to cast doubt on, an accepted interpretation is a valuable and original contribution to historical knowledge. This alone makes it worthwhile.

2.3 Museums

Using museums

Like Record Offices, museums are also useful to the student of history. These may be *national museums*, to which your school may organize a trip. Or you may wish to go yourself during holiday time to museums dealing in *specialist subjects* in which you have an interest, like the *Imperial War Museum*, where you could study recent changes in weaponry and in the conduct of modern warfare. There is the *National Railway Museum* in York, which is useful in comparing rail transport at the start of the twentieth century with that of the present time; the *National Motor Museum* in Beaulieu could be used for a similar purpose. Of course there are museums of a more *local character*, but which still deal with a specialist topic, like the *brewery museums* in Burton-on-Trent. These museums generally have useful collections of artefacts, backed by impressive photographic coverage of the subject, and a visit will almost certainly enable you to build up a useful collection of notes, as well as copies of the materials distributed by the museum. Your teacher will probably help you in working out a suitable subject for a coursework assignment in connection with the twentieth-century section of such museums.

Non-specialist municipal and county museums usually have good collections, though they will often deal with subjects far earlier than the twentieth century. Nevertheless, some will have a twentieth-century department, and may prove a valuable historical source. Local museums will also be especially valuable in providing material for a *local history assignment*, e.g. on conditions on the Home Front during the Second World War in the particular locality.

The tendency in museums is to move away from carefully-shielded displays in glass cases and towards what is sometimes called the 'hands-on experience'. That is to say, museum visitors are being increasingly invited to handle the exhibits and to get to know them by feel, instead of by studying them in the highly artificial context of a display cabinet. Thus, a Home Front collection might well include pots and pans, a fire range, a tin bath, a washboard and a carpet-sweeper for you to examine in detail, as well as copies of instruction pamphlets on air-raid drill, or photographs of women at work in munitions factories. There may be photographic coverage of the aftermath of air raids.

Cassette or filmstrip programmes sometimes accompany collections on a particular topic. They may be studied at the museum, or taken away on loan for more detailed study at your leisure. These can provide a good deal of material for a coursework assignment.

This *raw material* for history assignments, of course, needs further supporting information, perhaps from primary and secondary sources in the archive offices and libraries. Remember that the assignment you eventually produce will be a piece of *written work*, and that written resources, as well as artefacts, will be needed to complete it.

2.4 Historical fieldwork

> **Getting your feet wet**

It is sometimes said that it is a mistake to emphasise the use of *books* in the study of history at the expense of *boots*. Visits to local CROs may soon tempt you to turn from the situation as it exists in the records to that which exists on the ground. A comparison of two local maps in the record office, dating from 1910 and 1970 may make you think it would be a good idea to trace out the changes by *visiting* the areas illustrated; the closure of a local railway and its marking on the map as 'disused railway' may persuade you to walk along its former railbed and to take notes on it. Reading about slum clearance and rehousing in large towns may encourage you to visit both the cleared areas and the new areas of housing development. All this would be invaluable in supporting a local history assignment, such as some of those suggested above.

It is nearly always better to work *from* the records and *to* the visit, rather than the other way round. You may find that a very interesting visit has little archival support for further study. It is much more sensible to check on the materials available first, and then to make a visit in order to extend your knowledge.

Fieldwork may also be undertaken in more ambitious visits which your school may organize, perhaps to some useful historical site in the vicinity. Two such sites (to take random examples) are

- the *Durham Light Infantry Museum*, which provides information about the war service of the DLI in both world wars, with some of the letters the soldiers wrote to their families whilst they were abroad.
- the *former prisoner-of-war camp at Malton* in Yorkshire, now a museum telling the story of civilian life in the Second World War.

Fieldwork of a special kind could be used to support the projects mentioned above, namely *oral history*. Using a portable tape-recorder, you could interview elderly relatives or their friends and get them to answer questions, or to recount their experiences before the war, or during the blitz. A certain amount of forethought and planning is necessary here. More than one testimony is clearly preferable to a single one; indeed, the more the better. You should *discuss the proposal with your teacher*, and *plan a questionnaire* for the main points to be covered. Try to keep your witnesses to the point while they are answering, but at the same time avoid interrupting them too frequently, and try to talk as little as possible yourself. Oral history has the great value of immediacy, but it also has significant weaknesses: people may have forgotten what really happened, or, worse still, they may remember it only selectively, so that the final picture they paint may be misleading if not actually false. This is why *corroboration of recollected evidence* is so very important. In other words, this material needs further supporting information from *other sources* before it can be effectively employed in a coursework assignment.

Support for fieldwork projects and futher ideas on them may be found in a useful series published during the 1970s entitled *Field Studies for Schools*. Each booklet in the seven-volume series contains twenty or thirty suggestions for possible fieldwork in a given area of the country, though relatively few relate to twentieth-century subjects. Nonetheless, reading them may spark off some linked idea for fieldwork in your own period.

2.5 History games and computer programs

> **Going electronic**

A little thought will show you that as historical *evidence*, neither games nor computer programs are quite of the same order as the sources discussed above. Though they may be based on primary sources, both are in reality *manipulative techniques*. However, they are still valuable and important, and therefore ought to be included in this survey.

HISTORY GAMES

A number of publishers now produce a number of these history games, some of which are relevant to the demands of GCSE syllabuses. Broadly speaking, history games reproduce the main features of original historical situations, and create an opportunity for students to react to the problems that were faced and share in the decision-taking procedures of the period. In this way, students can view problems 'from the inside', and come to understand *why* the original participants in these decisions decided to act in the way they did. They can work out for themselves what the consequences would have been if the decisions taken had been different, and so create an alternative scenario, e.g. what might have happened if Hitler had *not* postponed the invasion of Britain in 1940. Students' decisions, taken on the evaluation of the evidence and by a process of negotiation, create a deeper understanding of the process of decision-taking.

Games naturally take the form of a *group activity*. In a situation such as that existing in Europe in 1938–39, a number of key roles will be identified, such as Daladier, Benes, Stalin, Chamberlain, Mussolini and Hitler, and those taking part in the game will be invited to re-negotiate their way through problems such as the Munich Crisis in order to see whether they can arrive at a more satisfactory outcome. Each player will have his own 'aims' and 'rules' in the game, and each will be seeking to secure particular objectives. Playing out the game will show to participants that the process of reaching a successful outcome is more complicated than they thought.

For a number of reasons, games and simulations cannot serve as coursework assignments in GCSE, but they *can* extend a group's understanding of the complexities of a historical problem. The hypothetical alternatives show that no particular outcome can be predicted with any certainty. This lessens the temptation – so evident in inexperienced students – to be 'wise after the event'.

COMPUTER PROGRAMS

Computer assisted learning packs are also commercially produced to help students of GCSE Modern World History. One such pack has the title *The Attack on the Somme*, and deals with this particular battle on the Western Front in the First World War. The program provides a historical replay in order to involve the student in the kind of decisions facing the military leaders and the soldiers on the battlefield in 1916, and their consequences. Another relates to *industrial management between the wars*, and explores the problems of making a cotton factory profitable in the changing economic climate. A third is called *Children on the Move*, and deals with the problems of the evacuation of children and their suitable billeting with reception families in the safe areas in 1939.

This type of simulation is similar to the history games outlined above, and shares a similar purpose – that of familiarising the student with the factors involved in decision-making in various situations. The programs also generally provide a good deal of supporting printed material in order to make possible some 'off-screen' work. Like history games, computer programs cast the student in an *active role* as a participant rather than as an observer; but unlike games, which are team experiences, computer programs are geared to the activities of *individual students*. Nonetheless, quite apart from the enjoyable experience of handling a computer, these programs serve the valuable function of increasing your understanding of the complexities of a particular problem, and of the variety of different solutions which may be produced to it.

Computer programs are also increasingly being used for *extracting specific information from masses of statistical material*. Those which extract birth rates or family sizes from censuses of population statistics, for example, will save the student the drudgery of sifting through mountains of figures, without lessening the importance of the task in hand. The time is fast coming when computers will be widely employed for mechanical tasks of manipulating existing information, freeing the historian to make new discoveries.

Before attempting to make use of either history games or computer programs, however, you should make sure that their use is permitted within the framework of the examination. Even if your teacher does not know the answer to this question, the Groups will certainly offer guidance on the subject to candidates. It would be foolish to employ either of them widely, only to find in the end that the regulations for the examination disallowed their use.

UNIT 3 METHODS OF INVESTIGATION

The assessment objectives and the sources of information discussed above are closely linked to the *methods of investigation* appropriate to the different types of history assignment in GCSE History.

3.1 Knowledge-based topics

Evaluation or assessment topics in GCSE History are mainly *knowledge-based,* as are empathy assignments. The methods to be adopted in such enquiries depend to an extent on the source of the information on which the knowledge is based.

BOOKS AND NEWSPAPERS

❝ Extracting the information ❞

The extraction of information from books and newspapers depends upon careful reading and note-taking. It is a means of extending the information provided by your teacher in the course of normal lessons. You should be careful to adopt the same good note-taking technique as you do for the rest of the course: keep your notes legible, write in ink to prevent rubbing or fading, and make intelligent use of headings, sub-headings and abbreviations. Make sure that you list all the main points rather than developing just one or two of them in unnecessary detail. Pick out with particular care those points that are obviously relevant to the subject of your enquiry. Try not to generate too much in the way of note material when you are embarking on a coursework project, especially not multiple accounts of the same event as it appears in different books. Try instead to slot your note material together, so that new information from later sources fits in neatly with the material you have built up already.

You may find that using different coloured inks or highlighting key words with a marker pen help to make your notes easier to use. Some people write their notes on one side of the paper only, so that the opposite blank page can be used for additions later culled from other texts. Notes may be arranged in the form of a diagram with linking arrows, or in tabular form, if this is more appropriate.

Books may be used several at a time; it is not essential that you should finish with one text before moving to the next. The useful thing about books and newspapers, of course, is that you can refer back to an earlier section if there is something you find you have forgotten or need to check again; the same is true of a tape recording, but you may find this less easy.

TV, SOUND BROADCASTS AND FILM

Unless you have the use of a video tape recorder, or unless you can actually run film through the projector again, the type of replay just mentioned is not available for other information media. You should therefore take rough notes as fast as you can during the programme, or, if it is too dark for that, as soon as possible afterwards, while the memory is still fresh in your mind. Where a recording device is being used, you may find there is a pause button which will enable you to produce good, thorough notes.

With broadcasts or with films, you may be watching or listening to the programme alone, or with the rest of your class. Conditions are likely to be more difficult with a group; but the compensation is that your teacher may well have worked out some way of helping you with the notes you have to make.

You may be asked to evaluate the programme's coverage of the subject. In this case it will be necessary for you to set it against the background of your other knowledge so as to be able to comment on its usefulness. Your comments will not be of an artistic character, since your task is that of the historian and not of the art critic. Whereas other films or TV broadcasts are often seen in isolation from one another, this, to be useful, must be seen in its historical context.

VISITS AND FIELD TRIPS

There are no action replays in this kind of historical activity, and your notes must be taken at the time, or very shortly afterwards. A spirally-bound notebook may be the best thing for your notes in this case, so that you can move easily from page to page, and a pencil may be better than a pen. You may find that sketches of the things you are looking at, built up into labelled diagrams, will be the best way of recording what you need. Don't forget that some of these observations will be taken in the open air (or even in the rain), and that the fewer loose papers you have the better.

Some sites may provide document packs of information, and may even suggest questions for you to follow up. If printed materials can be taken home, you may be saved a good deal of the writing that you would otherwise have to do at the time.

Sites are also useful for the empathetic experience they can produce. It is easier to understand how a prisoner-of-war felt in his camp, or a coal-miner felt in his cottage, when you have seen the conditions in which each of them lived.

3.2 Documentary assignments

> **How to deal with the documents**

In most cases you will not select the pieces of evidence for yourself, except possibly where it is local archival material relating to the project on which you are engaged. Normally an exercise of this sort will be given you by your teacher, and your skills will be revealed in your answers to the teacher's questions. Some of the skills which will be measured are:

- comprehension and interpretation
- evaluation.

COMPREHENSION AND INTERPRETATION

Comprehension

You must *know what the passages mean*. You must be familiar with their vocabulary, syntax and idiom. To assist you in comprehension, ordinary dictionaries are a help, at least as a starting point, with words such as 'plebiscite'. A number of words, however, like 'mandate' and 'sanctions', by their historical usage, have acquired almost a technical meaning, and this needs to be verified before you are confident of the meaning of the passage. Some of the vocabulary may be in a different language such as French (like 'détente') or German (like 'putsch'), or it may contain abbreviations which need to be expanded and understood. You have to be sure that the meaning you attach to a word is not just the one we use now, but the meaning that would have been usual at the time: even the word 'hopefully', which used to mean 'in an optimistic way', has in the last twenty years come to mean merely 'perhaps'. A passage may also contain difficult words conveying complicated concepts, such as 'totalitarianism' and you must understand the meanings of any such words.

Interpretation

There is more to understanding than vocabulary. You must also be able to grasp the author's intention in writing the passage, and to appreciate its shades of meaning – whether it is humorous, dismissive, ironic or patronising. From the author's choice of words you have to be able to judge the passage's tone. You have to be able to see it in the context of the problem with which it is dealing. Cartoons, speeches, letters, and even official documents may all have subtle hidden meanings. Nevertheless, care is needed here. Once more, you have to be sure that the meaning you attach to a phrase is not anachronistic, but is the meaning that would have been usual at the time: the words 'liquidate' and 'liquidation', for instance, originally taken from the vocabulary of bankruptcy, came to have the significance of 'destroy' or 'massacre', as in the statement 'the *kulaks*, and any others of his opponents whom he had reason to fear, Stalin sentenced to liquidation'. Later still the word was also used as a synonym for the word 'resolve' or 'fulfil', as in the statement 'We have liquidated all the objectives of our forward economic planning.' Other phrases may have been used in different ways by different people: phrases such as 'basic requirements for peace' have quite a different ring when heard from the mouth of Chancellor Kohl than when they were used by Adolf Hitler; and 'the rights of the rank-and-file of trade union members' sound quite different when applied to the strikers of 1926 than they do when the words are used by a Conservative politician of the 1980s. Thus interpretation goes further than vocabulary in revealing your grasp of a historical situation.

EVALUATION

You must not only understand the passages quoted, you must also be able to *weigh them up*. You have to ask yourself about:

- **Authenticity.** Is the document you are using genuine, or is it a *fake*? In some cases a document contains an obvious error that marks it down as spurious, but in other cases its origin is more doubtful, and has to be decided on the basis of probability, as with the 'Hitler Diaries'.

- **Reliability.** Can we be sure that the document is truthful in what it says? It may be that the author of the document was misinformed, or that he was prejudiced; perhaps he was simply lying. For a variety of reasons, it may be that we cannot put as much trust in the document as we should like. The writings of A.O. Avdienko, for instance, at the time of the Seventh Congress of the Soviets in 1935, have been criticised in this way because of their lyrical praise for the warmth and generosity of Stalin.
- **Validity.** Does the document prove what it is supposed to prove, or is it being used mistakenly to bear out an unwarrantable suggestion? For example, are all the anti-Communist statements put forward in *Mein Kampf* adequate proof of a Bolshevik plot to dominate the world, or are all the anti-American statements of the Ayatollah Khomeini over the shooting down of an Iranian airbus adequate proof of the savage and inhuman imperialism of the US Government?

In other words, there are three questions we should ask of any historical document:
1. Is it genuine?
2. Is it truthful?
3. Is it logically sound?

Please note that the answer to the first of these questions is quite scientific, and will take the form of a straight forward yes or no; but the answers to the other two are more subjective, and allow difference of opinion.

In addition, you have to be able to show your mastery of:

- **Analysis.** You have to be able to look at the component units of a document and see how it works, and how it achieves its effect. You have to be able to use the document to comment on the ideas of similarity and difference, change and continuity, and cause and consequence, any of which may be illustrated by it. You have to be able to decide whether it is sensible and closely-argued, or whether it is wild and far-fetched. You have to be able to deduce the extent to which it fits in closely with another document, or is at variance with it.
- **Bias.** You have to be able to detect bias, whether it occurs deliberately, as it usually does, or whether it occurs naturally and unconsciously. Bias must be distinguished from both *opinion* and from *judgment*. In the last two cases, the writer of the document is prepared to offer reasons for the view he takes, dissociating it from his personal emotions, but in the case of bias he offers no reasons for the view he takes, and presumes that everyone else will naturally share his assumptions. He frequently becomes heated and emotionally involved in the stance he thinks to be proper, and fails to deal fairly with opinions contradicting his own. Unconscious bias is very difficult to deal with, since it may not be easy to detect, especially when an audience holds similar views.
- **Inconsistency.** Documents may contain contradictions, or differing statements which cannot easily be reconciled with one another. You have to be able to identify these, and attempt to explain them. Sometimes the case is a simple one, as with figures in a table which fail to add up; in other cases, the inconsistency (where it exists) is more subtle, and needs more lengthy explanation. A statement from the Afrikaaner Nationalists, for example, may deny that South African troops are occupying the territory of their neighbours, but may go on to say that in the interests of national defence it has been necessary to station troops there.
- **Gaps.** Statistics may be missing from a table, relevant information from a statement, or logical steps from an argument. You have to be able to notice this, and to comment on the possible implications of the omission. Where an explanation is offered, you have to be able to say whether, in your opinion, it is adequate.
- **Extrapolations.** You have to make intelligent efforts to fill in any gaps that may exist in the evidence. For instance, if you were informed that the Jewish population of Palestine grew from 180,000 in 1932 to 400,000 in 1937, it would be reasonable to suppose that in 1935 it was somewhere between the two. There are limits, however, to the sort of extrapolations that can be made: it does not follow, for example, that since 10p pieces and £1 coins are circular, 20p and 50p pieces must be circular also.
- **Comparisons.** You should be able to compare two documents from the point of view of tone and factual content (see pages 11–12).

RESEARCH AND INVESTIGATION

The methods of investigation in all these cases of documentary assignment are very similar. In the case of documents which you have selected for yourself, they should illustrate the particular points which you wish them to demonstrate. In all other cases you should take care to:

1. Read and study the document closely. Close study is just as necessary with non-verbal material (photographs, pictures, cartoons) as it is with verbal extracts. Graphs and tables

must also be studied closely. You cannot answer detailed questions unless you are thoroughly familiar with the contents.

2. Each document should be provided with an *attribution*, i.e. you should be provided with the *name* of the author, the *date* of the extract and the *source* from which it is taken. The same is true of non-verbal material, e.g. cartoons, which may have the name of the artist, the date and the source of the cartoon, and may be provided with a caption. Tables and graphs should also acknowledge their sources. You should note these carefully, since you may need to make use of this information in the course of your answers.

3. Read the questions set on the document carefully, making sure that you have properly understood them before attempting your answer. In particular, check that you can answer every part of the question – do not be deceived by one or two easy 'openers' into thinking that the whole question is easy.

4. If a *mark tariff* is provided with the question, use this as a guide for how much you should write. If only 1 mark is on offer, a one-word or one-phrase answer will be adequate; anything more would be a waste of time. But if 6 or 8 marks are on offer, you will need to write more fully and to make a number of relevant points, so that you have a chance of reaching the maximum.

5. Work out roughly in your head the sort of material you ought to use in answering each component part. There is nothing worse than finding that you have 'over-written' an earlier answer, and have to repeat yourself in a later one. Putting 'ditto', or 'see (b) (ii) above' looks like lack of planning on your part.

6. If the question says 'Refer to the document . . .' or 'Use the document to show . . .' then make specific use of the document in your answer, quoting short passages as appropriate. Above all, do not ignore the document, relying on your memory to give the answer you think the question ought to have.

7. Use short quotations from the document if required to illustrate your points, but do not copy it out. If you use a quotation, indicate in your answer the point which it is meant to illustrate, e.g. the author's bias, sarcasm, ambiguity etc. Use quotation marks to indicate your quotation. Instead of copying out a quotation, line-number references may be used instead.

8. Do not overrun the time alloted for the question, but be equally sure that you do not write too briefly and so fail to do the question full justice.

MAKING THE BEST USE OF VISUAL MATERIAL

In carrying out coursework assignments, students do not always make the best use of the maps, photographs and cartoons which they may have; nor do they always use tables of statistics or graphs and other diagrams very successfully. This chapter is meant to offer you some guidance on how this may be done.

UNIT 1   MAPS, PHOTOGRAPHS AND CARTOONS

1.1 Maps

1   In using existing maps for tracing or for photocopying for purposes of a coursework assignment, be sure that you choose ones which are not too detailed or overcrowded. Black and white maps are generally better; if you need to have them coloured, it is often better to colour them yourself *after* the map is complete, and then in such a way that the information carried on the map is not obscured. In particular you should avoid maps which carry masses of information which are not needed for the purposes of the assignment. If the words are jumbled, or overlapping, or if they are written in such small print that they are not decipherable, then it is much better to aim for a simpler map.

In using a map that is *already drawn* you have to take into account its basic features if you are to avoid elementary errors:
a)   You have to know where 'North' is on the map. This is not only to avoid making simple mistakes such as reproducing the map upside-down, but to enable the person using the map to know the direction of surrounding features to the main subject matter of the map. If there is no north marker on the map, it is always a good idea to insert one.
b)   You have to know the scale of the map. This is something you have probably already learned in Geography, but this knowledge is not purely theoretical. It is very easy, for example, in comparing two land masses such as Cyprus and Sri Lanka to imagine that Cyprus is bigger simply because the map is on a bigger scale. In fact, Cyprus is only 3,500 sq. mls. in extent, whereas Sri Lanka is over 25,300 sq. mls. If there is no line scale at the bottom of the map, it is always a good idea to work one out and insert it.
c)   You have to remember that different projections give different ideas of land mass sizes, and even of shapes. You have probably also learnt this in Geography. The familiar Mercator projection has the effect of exaggerating land masses near the poles, so that places like Greenland and Australia look much bigger than they are. Looking at a Mercator projection, you would think that Greenland was nearly as big as Africa, whilst in fact it is only a fraction of the size. Try finding a map based on the *Peters* projection, which takes into account land areas.

How many of the faults listed above can you find on the map in Fig 3.1?

Try to select maps which contain simple, clear information relevant to the topic which you are considering, but which are not cluttered up with unnecessary information. If, for example, you were doing an assignment on the independence of India, you could do much worse than start with the map in Fig 3.2, adapted from one of the better-known map-book histories used in schools. This particular example lacks a scale and a north-pointer, and the 'Frontier of British India' should be marked with a heavy black line in the explanatory box, but otherwise the information it contains is concise and extremely useful.

2   Information may be carried in map form even on subjects which you would not automatically connect with a map presentation. In a sense, not all the information on them may be suited to maps, but such maps nonetheless have the advantage of putting together a large amount of information in a small space, saving a rather laborious textual presentation. The

Fig. 3.1 Map – example (1) from *The Serbs: Guardians of the Gate* R. G. D. Laffan (Oxford 1918)

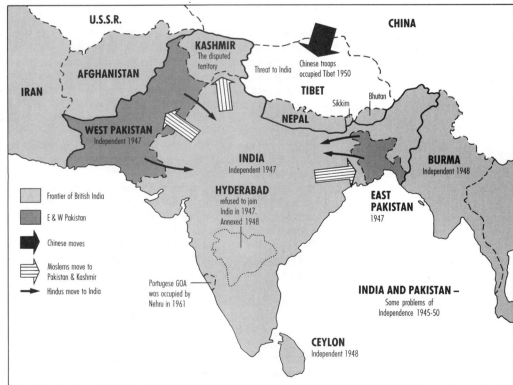

Fig. 3.2 Map – example (2) from *A Sketchmap History of the Modern World* Brian Catchpole (Heinemann 2nd Ed., 1974)

map opposite, on United States problems, is a good example. The most directly geographical part is the box in the bottom left corner; but the information carried on the flags in the upper part of the map is nonetheless well expressed and presented. Study the map, and see how many faults you can find in it.

3 Anyone who is familiar with the animated maps shown on film and television will recognize the importance of changes as revealed by the use of maps. Indeed, a comparison of the situations as shown on two closely similar maps is perhaps the best way of conveying information relating to territorial changes which have taken place during the interval between maps. As well as being the subject of possible questions in an examination, the

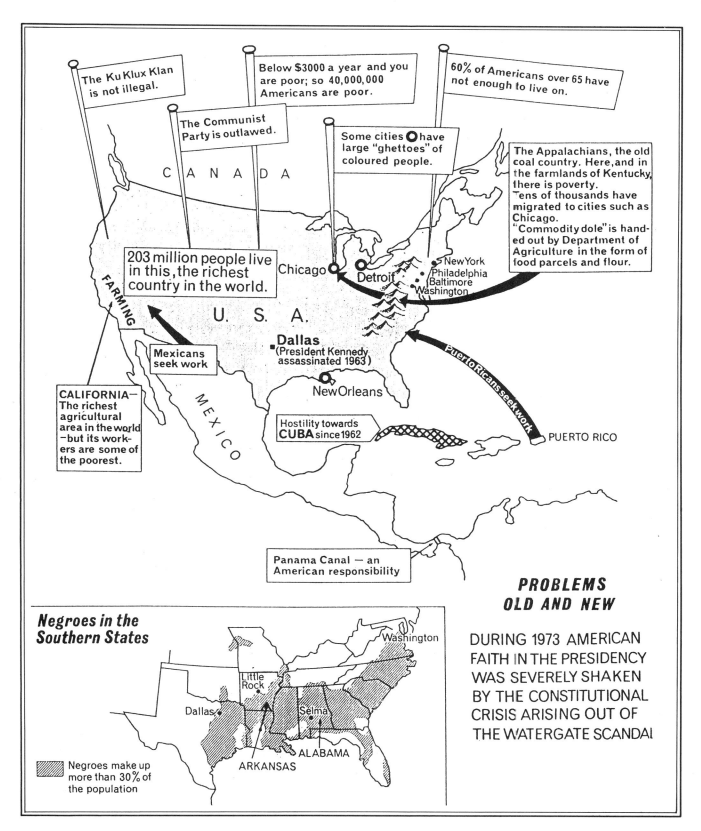

Fig. 3.3 Map example (3) from *A Sketchmap History of the Modern World* Brian Catchpole (Heinemann 2nd Ed., 1974)

use of more than one map to illustrate historical developments provides a useful technique for coursework assignments. Two examples are given below on pp 30–32.

The first example (Fig 3.4) is a map adapted from a book by Hugh Higgins (*The Cold War*, published by Heinemann) and illustrates the changes brought about by the Korean war, 1950–53.

Careful study of these maps and a thorough comparison between them will enable the student to reconstruct quite an accurate account of the war from the first North Korean invasion to the armistice of 1953. This sort of treatment is obviously much more full and informative than the kind of treatment given by the candidate who produced the single map used in Assignment 6.1 (on p. 65).

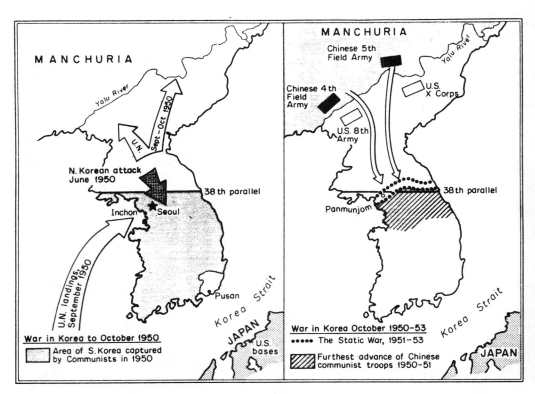

Fig. 3.4 Map – example (4) from *The Cold War* Hugh Higgins (Heinemann, 1984)

The second example (Fig 3.5) places a map adapted from D.G. Williamson's book *The Third Reich* (published by Longman) illustrating Europe at the height of Hitler's power alongside another from Hugh Higgins's book relating to the territorial arrangements in Europe at the time of the start of the Cold War (Fig 3.6).

Use of these two maps could save three or four pages of text describing verbally the political arrangements made for Nazi-controlled Europe about 1943, and comparing it with the arrangements made in 1945 after the collapse of the Nazi empire. A visual presentation of information not only has a greater immediacy and economy, but makes possible a point-by-point comparison for any area occurring on both maps. On a more practical level, the maps are both supplied with a clear explanatory key, and this is also of considerable assistance in grasping their meaning.

4 Before using maps that have already been drawn, it may be a good idea to discuss the matter with your teacher. Many teachers and examiners take the view that to use other people's maps is little better than using their words and sentences, and that doing so smacks of the 'scissors-and-paste' method which the GCSE examination is intended to discourage. They say that assignments are intended to test your abilities in history, and not the accuracy with which you can copy work from other people. Indeed, producing your own maps is undoubtedly better, not least because then you can control the nature and the extent of the information contained in them. But if you *do* produce your own maps, you must follow the same basic rules:

a) Your outline map may be somewhat simplified, but it must be basically *accurate*. Too many students produce maps which are either fussily over-complicated or else so badly drawn that there are no features of the map which may be recognized. To draw Europe as if it were egg-shaped or sausage-shaped is obviously too inaccurate, and counteracts any good that may be done by the information provided by it. If you look at the three maps supplied by the candidate who attempted Assignment 6.1 (p. 65) you ought to be able to work out how inaccurate these maps are. The size of Japan in Map 1, the omission of any countries between the Congo and Nigeria in Map 2, and the size and shape of all three countries in Map 3, reveals the very sketchy geographical knowledge on which these maps are based.

b) Your map should be supplied only with references *relevant* to the text; it is not a good idea to overload it with a mass of other information, since this is likely to obscure your meaning rather than to make it clear. You should take care, too, to ensure that the map is not merely a repetition of the information in the text; to express it in words, and then to repeat the information in map form adds little to the overall sense. A map is not intended solely as an ornament to improve the appearance of your work. The purpose of a map is to present the information in a rather different way eg, to reveal from the shape of the state of Israel some of the physical problems resulting from a long and difficult frontier,

CHAPTER 3 MAPS, PHOTOGRAPHS AND CARTOONS

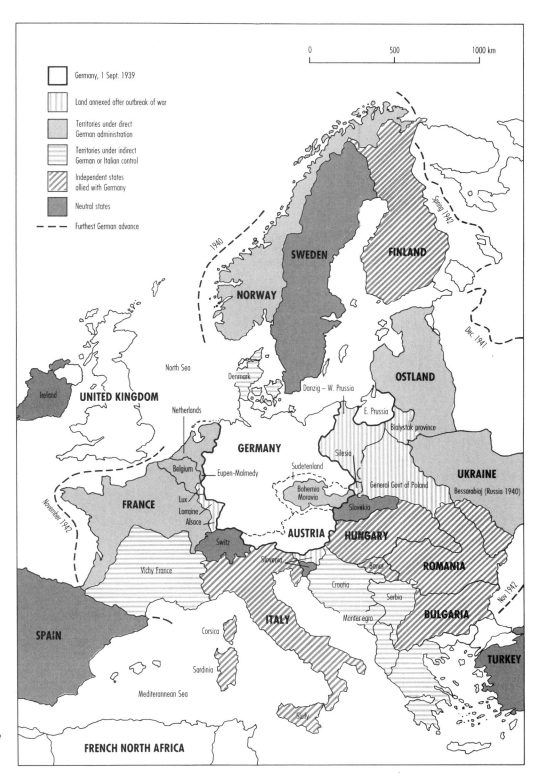

Fig. 3.5 Map – example (5) from *The Third Reich* D. G. Williamson (Longman, 1982)

and those resulting from strategical connecting corridors which are perilously narrow and open to attack.

c) It is necessary to mark in rivers and mountain ranges only when they make a positive contribution towards the map; but all your maps should be provided with a north pointer and an accurate scale for the reasons given above. If you decide to use colour for your map, do not allow it to obscure the meaning.

5   However, the maps involved in an assignment may simply be given to you as part of the assignment, and then the question of copying them or reproducing them does not arise. You are often asked questions on a variety of different historical sources, one of which may be a map. These questions, amongst other things, may invite you to interpret the maps, to compare them with the other sources that are supplied, or to offer your comments on what maps contain and what they omit. You may be asked about the date

Fig. 3.6 Map – example (6) from *The Cold War* Hugh Higgins (Heinemann, 1984)

and the source of a map, and even to judge whether it is a purely factual document, as many maps are, or whether it hides some propagandist intention.

None of these things is easy to do without practice, but the skill, like most skills, can be acquired over a period of time by appropriate exercise. Let us take Fig 3.6, for instance, and consider it as part of an exercise alongside other documentary material. Two documents, such as those which follow, may be selected and presented to you as part of a coursework assignment.

Extract 1

line 1   From Stettin on the Baltic to Trieste in the Adriatic, an iron curtain has descended across the continent. Behind that line lie all the capitals of the ancient states of Central and Eastern Europe . . . The Communist parties, which were very small in all these eastern states of Europe, have been raised to pre-eminence and power far beyond their numbers and are

line 5   seeking everywhere to obtain totalitarian control. Police governments are prevailing in nearly every case, and so far, except in Czechoslovakia, there is no true democracy.

(Speech of Winston Churchill at Fulton, Missouri, 1946)

Extract 2

Stalin's choice was whether his long-term ideological and national interests would be better served by a short-run truce with the West or by an immediate resumption of pressure. In October 1945 Stalin indicated . . . that he planned to adopt the second course – that the

line 10   Soviet Union was going isolationist. No doubt the succession of problems with the United States contributed to this decision, but the basic causes most probably lay elsewhere: in the developing situations in Eastern Europe, in Western Europe, and in the United States.

(Arthur Schlesinger, Jr., in Origins of the Cold War, 1967)

Apart from questions on the documents themselves – perhaps relating to their authorship, their dating, their language and meaning, and evaluative questions such as how far they are in agreement – questions may also be asked in relation to the map. What evidence is there in the map to *support* the documents? The map clearly shows that certain areas have been annexed by Russia, the others are 'dominated by communist regimes imposed by Stalin' (if the key of the map is to be believed), and that yet others are Russian 'occupation zones'. In short, the map seems to share the same anti-Soviet *bias* as the two written documents. But there are certain things which a map cannot indicate. It does not indicate the existence of any sort of 'iron curtain'; it merely indicates a frontier. It has nothing to say about the size of the communist parties in the eastern European states; it does not reveal the existence of totalitarian control; it does not show any 'police states', and it reveals no lack of democracy, 'true' or otherwise. In point of fact, it does not even show a frontier 'from Stettin to Trieste', let alone an iron curtain.

Maps are also incapable of revealing the existence of Stalin's motives in his actions towards eastern Europe; all they show is the result of the events in that part of the world. So the map can have nothing to say about a 'short-run truce' or an 'immediate resumption of pressure'. Nor can it say whether the Soviet Union was 'going isolationist'. It says nothing about 'basic causes', and casts no light on the 'problems of eastern Europe' – nor, of course, on those of other areas not shown on the map.

Nevertheless the information on the map is interesting and is useful up to a point in bearing out the message of the two documents. It shows that, for whatever reason, a large area of central and eastern Europe had passed into Soviet control, which formed an important part of what Churchill was saying. It shows that this control in some cases amounted to outright annexation, irrespective of what the peoples of Latvia, Estonia etc., may have thought. It shows that some areas further west were garrisoned by the Soviet Union, whose powers there were direct and military. And it shows that five or six eastern European countries were ruled by communist governments, which may or may not have been directed by Moscow. There can be no denying that this Soviet advance constitutes a considerable change in the situation as it existed either before the war or at the height of the war in 1942.

1.2 Photographs

Photographs are a good way to give greater vividness and immediacy to your work, so long as they are relevant, well-chosen and not so numerous that they swamp the text. They should also be capable of being reproduced well. Too many assignments are spoiled by dark, fuzzy photographs which may have looked acceptable in the original but, because they are soft-focus, or because they are taken in colour, do not copy crisply. Perhaps the best way of knowing whether they will copy well is by trying to copy them. If they do not, there is not a lot that can be done – you could try a larger or more expensive copier, but even these have their limitations.

Selecting photographs is not merely done on account of their artistic qualities. The best photographs will bring out some point made in your text, or will clarify a point which needs visual illustration to put across. For example, the photograph in Fig 3.7 can be used very powerfully to support your text. It points up the flimsy, makeshift character of the Berlin Wall; it stresses the conditions of urban squalor and dreariness in which many Berliners lived; it emphasizes the contrast between the busy, crowded side on the right and the empty street on the left, without traffic and practically deserted except for a guard with a rifle. Which side is the photograph taken from? Why is this significant, and how does it affect the message which the photograph is meant to convey?

Fig. 3.7 Photograph – example from *International Affairs* E. G. Rayner (Arnold, 1984)

You can perhaps begin to understand the varied uses which can be made of the art of photography. You should be sceptical of the view often asserted that 'the camera cannot lie'. Perhaps it does convey the literal visual truth of the moment, but there may be serious doubts about its reliability.

Photographs may portray an *untypical* moment quite unrepresentative of the general situation. You may see a group of enthusiastic Poles welcoming Hitler in a town on the Eastern Front; but there may be crowds of others who are not shown who took a vastly different view. You may see the streets of Vienna lined with cheering Austrians showering Hitler with flowers as he entered the city in 1938; but this does not prove that he was universally welcome there. You may see groups of Hungarians sitting through a party meeting in the early 1950s, and be told that they are applauding and cheering; but the fact that they have their mouths open may show they are yawning from boredom rather than shouting with approval. A photograph snatched in a single moment may give a quite different and untrue impression of what a situation really was over a period of time.

In a real sense, too, perhaps the camera can be *made* to lie. Scenes can be posed, and the people appearing in them may be actors in costume playing a part rather than real people. Even if they are real, their actions can be manipulated by the photographer: he may suggest that they do this or that, or wear a particular expression on their faces. Their whole behaviour may be designed as a public relations exercise rather than as actuality. Artificial behaviour is seen at its most unreal in party political commercials, which are in fact nothing other than advertising matter.

Furthermore, existing photographs can be cleverly *tampered with*, using the skill of the artist who 'touches up' a photograph to give a quite deliberately untrue account of what actually took place. If you believe that the camera cannot lie, you should consider how the Czechoslovakian authorities altered a key photo for their purposes. One, published in 1968, gave a truthful picture of events in Czechoslovakia in that year, and showed Alexander Dubcek in front of a group of people in Prague, most of whom seem to be his supporters; the other, published afterwards and skilfully doctored, showed the same scene – but this time with Dubcek edited out. Only a very close examination of the second photograph would have enabled you to 'spot the join'.

The greatest care should be taken with photographic illustrations; they should be carefully selected, and should give as truthful an account of what they depict as you are able to find; they should be inserted at the appropriate point in the text to make their point most effectively; they should be clear and crisp; *there should not be too many of them*, for fear that your assignment begins to look like a scrapbook.

Photographs, too, like maps, can also be used in conjunction with documents in comparative and evaluative assignments. Figure 3.7, for example, could easily be put alongside other evidence dealing with the construction of the Berlin Wall, and questions asked on it. For example, the document might read as follows:

line 1   Action came early on Sunday, August 13th. Armoured cars rolled up to the border. Police and soldiers sealed all but twelve of the eighty crossing points and by morning sprawling spirals of barbed wire had cut the city in two.

line 5   The three Western commandants were told by West Berlin's mayor, Willy Brandt, that East Germany had taken over East Berlin and destroyed the city's four-power status. It was a direct act of aggression which demanded retaliation.

Thousands gathered on the border, angry and frustrated as the barricade of wire thickened. Many took advantage of their own freedom to come to see for themselves the Russian tanks and lorries which had turned the other side into an armed camp.

line 10   On Wednesday, 250 000 people gathered in front of West Berlin's City Hall, frightened and angry, bearing posters reading "Munich, 1938; Berlin, 1961". Brandt said he had requested immediate action from Kennedy – an act dismissed by Americans as rude and unscrupulous. But Kennedy was increasingly unhappy. Some Bonn students sent him a black umbrella, symbol of Chamberlain and his appeasement policy. He decided on action and sent Vice-

line 15   president Johnson to head a special mission to Berlin. With him went General Clay, the hero of the airlift. The US garrison, too, was to be reinforced. The West was going to stand firm.

(John Man, *The Coming of the Wall*, 1968)

You can see that to some extent the document bears out the images of the photograph, but, like a map, there are only a limited number of inferences that you can make. In particular, the document represents a *narrative*, taking place over a period of time of at least a number of days; but you have to remember that the photograph is a single *moment* of time, frozen for ever on the photographic plate. It can tell you how things looked at that particular moment, but it cannot tell you what people felt like, nor what their leaders were doing and saying at the time. You will note that the Wall itself is not mentioned in the document, though there are two mentions of barbed wire. The photograph and the extract also have different dates – what bearing would you say this would have on any comparison between them?

Nevertheless the two have a clear historical value, and provide a general corroboration for each other; there is certainly no contradiction between them. Further pieces of evidence, if they were provided, would help to shed still more light on this episode in history.

1.3 Cartoons

Apart from their use in examination papers, cartoons can provide useful illustrations appropriate to your assignment work. They often contrive to put across their message very pithily, and are frequently, thought not always, amusing. Cartoons, also, can express quite subtle shades of meaning, something that would be difficult to put briefly in words; they can, furthermore, express pictorially ideas which seem too brutal or too impolite to go into words. If you were actually to say out loud some of the things which are suggested in them, you would probably find yourself in court on a charge of slander – if nothing worse! When drawn in wartime to deal with the nation's enemies, they can not only portray the other side's leaders very cruelly, but can make suggestions which sound altogether too bombastic or chauvinistic to be expressed verbally.

Let us take a cartoon by one of Britain's greatest cartoonists, David Low (Fig 3.8). Study this cartoon for a while, and work out what you think it has to say, before turning to the comments that follow.

Fig. 3.8 Cartoon – example (1) from *Years of Wrath* David Low (Gollancz)

"DUCE! DUCE!"

The cartoon deals with relations between two states which were enemies to Britain at the time of the Second World War.

a) Which were these states? They are shown to be Italy and Germany. How can we tell? On the left, rising from the back of the chair, is the axe and the bound bundle of rods that served as one of the symbols of Italian Fascism; hanging up alongside is Mussolini's hat. On the right a group of figures, three of whom wear military uniform, and with their hands held high in a Nazi salute. Both sides of the cartoon represent fairly conventional stereotypes of the two nations Britain was fighting.

b) Are any of the figures recognizable? At the front of the group of men on the right, wearing black gloves, is Hitler, his Iron Cross on his chest. To his left, not in uniform, but wearing a light-coloured jacket and black trousers, is Josef Goebbels, his propaganda minister. Why do you suppose he is represented as a dwarf? Note what is said above about the unspeakable inference often seen in cartoons – how do you explain that you cannot call an opponent a dwarf, or a cripple, though you can draw him as one? The cartoon seizes on one notable feature of Goebbels – mainly that he was short – and exaggerates this feature in order to make Goebbels appear a more ridiculous and insignificant figure than he really was. Low's 'belittling' of Goebbels is not just figurative; it is literal.

c) How is Mussolini portrayed? What has happened to his head and his hands? Has he been shot to pieces at close range, so that his chair is spattered with his blood? Or is he simply a straw man, with his stuffing poking out of his collar and his cuffs? If you look at the ends of his trousers, you will see the answer. They have been tied up, so as to prevent his stuffing from leaking out. The answer is that he seems to be a military uniform, stuffed with straw.

d) What does the cartoon mean? The figures on the right are grotesque, too unintentionally comic to be really threatening; but an element of menace still remains. But poor Mussolini is quite pathetic. He would never frighten anyone. The whole message is a jibe at Mussolini's expense: he is totally inadequate, full of bombast and boasting, and in the end nothing more than a stuffed dummy. One way to make people feel better about their enemies is to make cruel fun of them, whether or not there is a shred of truth in what is being said; and this is Low, clearly doing his bit for the war effort by jeering at the nation's foes.

Now do the same with this second cartoon. There are obvious differences here, and the

CHAPTER 3   MAPS, PHOTOGRAPHS AND CARTOONS

Fig. 3.9   Cartoon – example (2) from *Years of Wrath* David Low (Gollancz)

raucous insult of the wartime cartoon is absent; but there is a clear political message all the same. Before looking at the comments below, can you work out the cartoon's meaning, and suggest which of the figures in the cartoon is portrayed more sympathetically than the others? The artistic qualities of the two cartoons could be contrasted by an art historian, the former being aggressive and strident, the second a quieter and more thoughtful cartoon; but it is not so much art evaluation as historical evaluation which the student will be expected to produce.

a) Who are the four figures on the left, shown sitting in chairs? In case there should be any doubt, their names are given in the border at the foot of the cartoon. Why do you suppose that Low has given the names of Hitler and Mussolini, when he does not do so in the wartime cartoon? You may conclude that the two other figures, Chamberlain and Daladier, were less visually recognizable (even at the time) than were the more famous pair; so that it is safer to name all of them in order that the cartoon may be properly understood.

b) Why are they shown sitting in a group round a globe of the world? This is to suggest that, as the statesmen they are supposed to be, they are dealing with world affairs, and are resolving some diplomatic problem.

c) Why is there a map on the wall behind them? The map shows Czechoslovakia, and helps to suggest that it is with Czechoslovak questions, rather than with the world as a whole, that they are dealing in their negotiations.

d) In the doorway, and scratching his chin, is the booted figure of Joseph Stalin, and the caption to the cartoon tells us the question which he is supposed to be asking as he walks into the room. Why do you think he is concerned that there is no place for him at this conference?

e) Can you date the cartoon? The four figures in solemn enclave, and the discussions over Czechoslovakia should all point to September 1938, which was the occasion of the Munich conference on the Sudetenland question.

f) What is the meaning of the cartoon? Stalin is surprised at being left out of the Munich discussions, and asks why he has not been invited. Why is this? He was certainly one of those who jointly guaranteed the independence of Czechoslovakia in 1935, and therefore, you might suppose, had very good reason to be present; but the other powers were anti-communist and were deeply suspicious of Soviet intentions. They would rather settle the matter without reference to him than give him his due share in the proceedings. Low seems to suggest that Stalin *should* have had a place at Munich.

g) Where do Low's sympathies lie? Chamberlain and Daladier both look blank, being politicians and professionally inscrutable. Hitler looks very smug, undoubtedly pleased to have got away with his Sudetenland deal without Russian interference. Mussolini, arms folded, plays his usual dramatic role to obtuse perfection. Only Stalin, with his puzzled smile, gets faintly sympathetic treatment from the cartoonist.

As in the cases of the map and the photograph used as examples in the first two sections of this Unit, this Munich cartoon might also be used in a comparative or evaluative assignment alongside a Munich document. The sharp comment of the Soviet Foreign Minister to the

French Ambassador to the USSR, written shortly after the Munich Conference, might provide such a document:

line 1   I said that in the light of the recent events it became easier to explain the strange phenomenon that the French, having concluded with us a Pact of Mutual Assistance, had systematically evaded discussing military matters concerning methods of carrying out that assistance. It now had to be concluded that the French government had never intended to render the assistance
line 5   envisaged by the pacts and that therefore it had seen no need to go into a detailed discussion about methods.

(From Ministry of Foreign Affairs of the USSR, 1938–39, Litvinov)

Again, it can be seen that to a large extent the cartoon and the document bear out each other's message, and provide each other with effective corroboration. Nevertheless it has to be remembered that the document is an official record from the Foreign Ministry archives and is based upon privileged information and special personal knowledge, whereas the cartoon, coming from the pen of a journalist working for a British newspaper, is totally of a different order. It would be dangerous to read too much into the similarity.

Here is a third cartoon by the same artist. Perhaps by this time you can answer the questions with a little more self-confidence.

Fig. 3.10 Cartoon – example (3) from *Years of Wrath* David Low (Gollancz)

TWO'S COMPANY, BUT THREE'S MORE COMFORTABLE

a) Who is sitting in the middle of the settee? Again in uniform though no longer in jackboots, we can recognize Stalin.
b) Who are the female figures? They are in national costume, but in case we should not recognize them, they each wear their appropriate label.
c) Why is Stalin inviting one of them, the rather doubtful-looking figure of Poland, to sit beside him? Using the analogy of the Christmas party to give an everyday meaning to his political message, Low seems to say that the Soviet Union finds security in being flanked by friendly eastern European states, and would like to be surrounded by them.
d) Can you date the cartoon? Since the portrayal is understanding and friendly, the date must come before the Cold War developed in 1946 (unless we know that Low was a communist sympathiser – which he was not). The date must be towards the end of the

war, if the two named eastern and central European states are now free to choose their friends. Since clearly Stalin has not yet imposed on Poland a communist regime meeting with his approval – something that happened towards the end of 1944 – the cartoon probably dates from the later part of 1943.

All of these cartoons, of course, may be used in an appropriately chosen assignment. At the same time, you ought to be careful not to read too much into the meaning of a cartoon, but give it proper objective treatment. What are the particular values of a political cartoon?

a) As in the case of empathy, we must recognize that people in the past had clear opinions of their own, but that their opinions at the time may have been different from our own at present. We may therefore learn something from a cartoon about popular attitudes at the time which we may not have known already.

b) But we must not suppose that everyone thought the same way as the cartoonist, for the cartoon was drawn by him alone, and not by the general public. He was expressing his personal point of view.

c) Perhaps a cartoon, therefore, has very little value, if it speaks only for the opinions of the cartoonist. But, cartoonists have a habit of reaching down into people's feelings and guessing what they are thinking. If we say that it is a *great cartoon* what do we mean then? We mean that whether everyone agreed with it or not, it struck a chord in the popular mind; people may not have agreed with it, but they thought the comment was appropriate and deserved to be uttered. So cartoons *do* give us an insight into the public mind at the time that they were drawn.

Cartoons, however, are not always as explicit as the examples used so far. It may not in fact be easy to say with any accuracy what any cartoon means. One final example will perhaps serve to make us a little wary about over-using them.

Fig. 3.11 Cartoon – example (4) from *The Guardian* by Gibbard

'*Young man! I am warning you.*'

a) Outside the ring we see Alec Douglas Home, British Foreign Secretary and one of the leaders of the Conservative Party, shouting to the wrestler poised on the top rope of the ring. Home is dressed as an angry old lady, and is furiously waving his umbrella and his handbag. The words of the caption tell us what he is shouting.

b) Other figures outside the ring are more difficult to recognize, though one of them towards the right of the front row may be US President Richard Nixon, looking indignant and concerned.

c) The figure on the top rope has a black eye-patch and the Jewish Star of David on the front of his wrestling costume. He seems to be intended as Moshe Dayan, the controversial

Israeli War Minister at the time. Having thrown his Arab opponent out of the ring completely, he is about to jump into the ringside seats himself to polish him off.
d) The referee inside the ring is an appropriately garbed skeleton and symbolizes death. The struggle between the Jews and the Arabs, evidently, is not so light-hearted as you might think from this picture.
e) What is the date of the cartoon? To which Arab-Israeli war does it refer?
f) Whose side does the cartoonist take? Does he mean that the Americans are helpless bystanders? Does he think that the British Foreign Secretary is a silly old woman? Does he feel sorry for the Arabs? Does he think that Moshe Dayan is a courageous little hero or a homicidal maniac? The whole cartoon might seem a suitable comment on the international situation at that time – if we only know what it meant.

Undoubtedly the best cartoons to use in your work are those whose meanings are the most plain. But you must take care not to introduce anachronisms into your work by attributing to cartoonists ideas and intentions which were far from their minds at the time. In the same way, if the cartoon has been selected for you and an exercise set upon it, you must be careful in deducing the political meaning from the drawing. You might, for example, draw some disastrous conclusions if you thought that the Gibberd cartoon above was from the Six Days War of 1967, and not from the Yom Kippur War of 1973. On the other hand you could be forgiven for not knowing that the cartoon actually dated from September 1972 and referred to the tough Israeli line taken with the Arabs by Dayan in 1972, a year before the Yom Kippur War broke out, rather than to the war itself in the autumn of 1973.

It should finally be pointed out (as has already been hinted) that there may be a strong propagandist element in any of these media – maps, photographs or cartoons; and this may be the subject of a history question. As well as lying by including false information, maps may lie by omission – ie by leaving out information which, if they were impartial, they would include. Their information is *selective*, and may be slanted to suit the interests of the person or group which issued them. The same is obviously true of photographs, whether they are stills, or the moving pictures of the cinema and the television. No one should underestimate the enormous potential for propaganda in the editing of film or television material; it is really only ignorance on the part of human beings, who fancy that because it has been photographed it must therefore be true, that allows this potential to go largely undetected. Cartoons, also, have a strong propagandist element – it could be argued that they are almost exclusively propaganda. Whether the cartoonist is trying merely to propagate his own views, or whether he is serving some higher political authority which is instructing him on how he ought to make people think, it cannot be denied that, with the aid of his pictorial images (always more easily memorable than words) he is largely influencing people's minds.

The same is true of the other forms in which information is presented: statistics, graphs and diagrams. These too can easily serve a propaganda purpose.

UNIT 2 STATISTICS, GRAPHS AND DIAGRAMS

2.1 Statistics

Figures may readily be used to quantify statements made in the course of your assignment. If you are referring to military expenditure under the Nazis, or the numbers and equipment involved in the Soviet army, or the amount of unemployment or the extent of inflation in Western Europe since the Second World War, it is useful to be able to bring out figures to prove the point being made. Generalizations that are unsupported by factual evidence may be irritating rather than enlightening, for there are limits to what you can expect people to accept purely on trust.

Before you use statistics, you must be sure to get them right. You may take them whole from a single source, in which case it should not be difficult to ensure that they are constructed on a comparable basis; or you may adapt them from a variety of different sources, in which case you may have trouble expressing the figures comparably. A very simple example is railway mileage – in Britain it will be expressed in miles, but in France in kilometres. Before you can make any meaningful comparisons, you have to express these lengths in common units, either miles or kilometres. If you are examining population growth, say for the United Kingdom, you will have to be sure that you are comparing like with like. You may find that some figures are for England and Wales, others for Great Britain, and others for the whole of the British Isles. You will have to be sure that the statistics deal with the same thing. Some statistics, for instance from developing countries, do not count still-births in the population figures, but you will find that European countries do, and then they add the deaths to the infant mortality figures. You have to be careful to see what is included in the category you are examining, and how consistently it is measured (whether it is motor-car output, steel exports or imports of foreign woollens) before you offer figures which are really comparable.

Likewise you have to be careful with your sources, preferring those which appear to be the most reliable, and, in the case of conflict between them, relying on the version which seems to be the most authoritative or best supported. You should make a note of where your figures are from, and whether you constructed the table yourself from different sources, or whether you adapted the table from a single source. When you use a table in your work, always be sure to attribute it to the correct source so that, if need be, it can be checked later. A set of figures that defy verification are of very little value to a historian.

If you are supplied with figures in an assignment, you have furthermore to be sure that you are reading and using them correctly. Let us take the imaginary statistics given in Figure 3.12 and 3.13 as a suitable instance.

Fig. 3.12 Statistics – example (1): Selected items of W. German industrial output (quinquennial averages)

Product & units	1955	1960	1965	1970	1975
Steel (m. tons)	8.4	10.2	12.7	9.3	11.9
Machine tools (000 units)	0.8	1.1	1.5	0.9	1.4
Turbines (m. kWh)	1.0	1.6	2.3	1.1	1.9
Locomotives (units)	477	587	404	277	205

Fig. 3.13 Statistics – example (2): Selected items of UK power output

Product & units	1950	1960	1970	1980
Crude oil (m. tons)*	–	–	35.7	309.8
Coal (m. tons)*	176.3	155.9	100.8	104.7
New nuclear power stations†	2	3	0	7

*Average figures for the decade
†Total for the decade

How can we read these figures? The whole of the first table (Fig 3.12) is supposed to be expressed in *quinquennial averages*, that is, the totals for each of the five years in each column added together and then divided by five, to give an average over the five years; this is better than plucking out a year at random. Then the top line of this table gives us steel production in million tons. So we can see that in 1955 West Germany is said to have produced 8 400 000 tons of steel. In the case of machine tools, we have the figure of 0.8 of a thousand units – ie 800 units. We have turbines generating 1 million kilowatt hours, and there are 477 single locomotives. Various things may strike you about these figures: there seems to be a downward dip in 1970 in output figures, and you may wonder what the reason was; the figures of machine tool production may seem altogether too low, unless *machine tool* is being used to describe only very large machine tools; and the figures for locomotive production may seem very high, though their steady decline seems consistent with the decline of the railways. What you cannot do with these figures, of course, is to *add them together*, since they are expressed in quite different units, and their totals would be meaningless.

The lower table (Fig 3.13) also contains a number of points. The first two rows of figures are average figures for the decade; that is, they are calculated as above, but over a ten-year average instead of five. But the bottom row is the total figure for the decade; in other words between 1950 and 1960, three nuclear power stations were opened. Here you should notice the difference between the dash (–) in the first two columns and the zero (0) in the third row. The dashes mean 'only an insignificantly small amount' of say, 35 tons, or 1350 tons; whereas in the third line '0' means actually 'none', ie no new nuclear power stations were opened between 1960 and 1970. Dashes also mean 'there are some figures, but I don't know what they are'. If oil output, in million barrels, was said over three years to be:

$$270 \quad - \quad 340$$

this would not mean that the middle figure was an 'insignificant amount', perhaps it was quite a substantial amount, but we don't know what it is. Thus, a gap in figures means that we do not know, or that we *do* know the amount and it is *too tiny to bother about*; whilst '0' actually means 'zero'.

These are all quite straightforward points, but tables of figures can become very complicated. The one in Fig 3.14 is not quite as complicated as the original from which it is adapted, but it still shows some of the difficulties and dangers of using figures.

Fig. 3.14 Statistics – example (3): Selected agricultural output (1964)

Crop	Yields per acre (bushels)		USSR as % of USA	Production (000 bushels)		USSR as % of USA
	USA[1]	USSR[2]		USA[1]	USSR[2]	
Corn, grain	62.6	27.8	44	3,583,800	362,200[4]	10
Wheat	26.3	12.6	48	1,290,650	2,121,000[4]	164
Rye	19.5	12.1	62	33,000	504,000[4]	1,152
Oats	43.1	19.1	44	880,000	269,000[4]	31
Barley	37.9	20.4	54	403,000	1,093,000[4]	271
Grain sorghum	41.1	(5)		492,000	(5)	

(1) US Department of Agriculture (USDA): Area harvested
(2) Derived
(3) USSR Statistics
(4) USDA Estimate
(5) Not available

We see first of all that these are comparative figures, and that they compare US and Soviet agricultural output. If the figures are published by an American source (as they are), there may be some initial scepticism about their reliability, since the source may have some ulterior motive in producing them. But there are other problems. We may not know what some of the categories are, eg 'Corn, grain' or 'Grain sorghum'. This is a fairly familiar problem, and not a disastrous one. But we also see, according to footnote (1), that in the case of the US figures we are looking at areas harvested. This would seem to be reasonable, since you cannot calculate yields from areas that have not been harvested – yet the same does not seem to apply to the Soviet figures. Why is this? The Soviet figures, furthermore, according to footnote (2), are said to be 'derived'. What does this mean? Is it that we know the area under cultivation, and the total output, and have simply worked out the figure for output per acre for ourselves? Footnote (3) gives us a slight pause – since we cannot find (3) in the table, there do not actually seem to be any Russian figures here *at all*. Instead, many of the important statistics in this table seem to be no more than US estimates. This could seriously weaken the value of the table. Indeed, in the sixth (last) row of the table *no* Soviet figures are given, and the table would therefore seem to be valueless as a basis for comparison. You have to bear all these factors in mind in reading a table of statistics, especially if you are going to draw any conclusions from it.

In the light of this example, it is scarcely necessary to point out the propaganda potential of figures. It was Thomas Carlyle who once said that 'you can prove anything by figures'. The newspapers are regularly full of ways in which people, and even governments, can manipulate statistics to give them the appearance they desire. Thus, in your work, you ought to look very carefully at figures, not only to find out whether they are credible, but also to see the basis on which they have been constructed – particularly whether this basis has been changed in the course of the table. Inflation figures and cost of living figures are two cases in point. When looking at inflation statistics, you should always observe what the *base year* is; if you are looking at figures whose base year is 1985 you will have modest increases of something like 12%; but if the base year is 1950 the increases will be well over 100%. Cost of living figures should also be handled carefully; you have to know what goes to make up these figures, and, more significantly, what has been left out. If the items omitted have seen the biggest price-rises of all, we have to ask whether their omission is not deliberately intended to keep the figures low.

2.2 Graphs and diagrams

Information can be presented in ways other than tables of figures. The illustration opposite gives you a number of these ways.

The first is known as a *pie chart*. It shows a circle cut into slices of appropriate size in order to show the relative sizes of the various continents. This chart is a useful device, and can be quite accurate; but unless you are prepared to use a protractor for measuring the angles accurately, the chart will give you only a pictorial idea of the quantities involved. The second is called a *bar graph*, and quantifies the actual sizes of the continents in million square miles. It is thus more factual, and perhaps more useful than a pie chart. The third is a different kind of bar diagram, with the bars running the other way. Can you read for yourself the information which this bar graph is giving you? What does it mean, for instance, when the third column rises higher than the second? And what is the difference between the information given in columns for 6 and 7 goals, and the column for 8 goals? The fourth diagram is a *graph*. A graph is usually drawn on squared paper, and is formed by a continuous line quantified along two different

CHAPTER 3   **STATISTICS, GRAPHS AND DIAGRAMS**   43

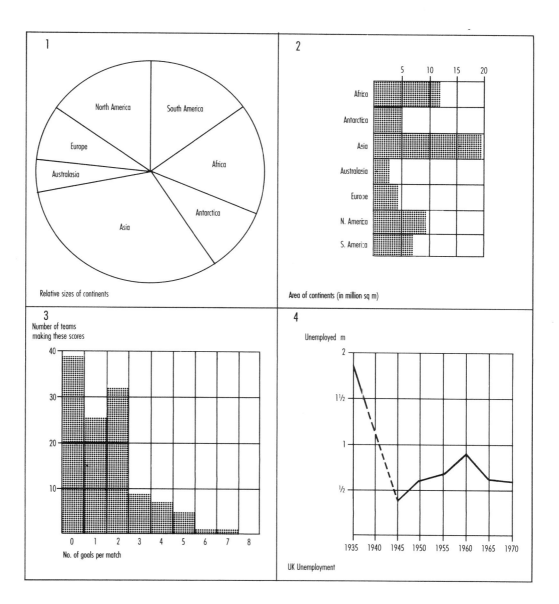

Fig. 3.15   Graphs and diagrams – example (1)

axes. This graph tells us the number of people who were unemployed in the years between 1935 and 1970, not year by year, but in quinquennial periods. A more detailed graph can, of course, be produced on an annual basis, but a quinquennial one is probably accurate enough. What do you suppose the dotted line between 1940 and 1945 means? Is the answer that we simply do not know? What other answer can there be? You may think that it is misleading to connect the two ends with a dotted line – perhaps it would be better simply to leave a gap in the line.

There are many ways in which graphs and diagrams, like tables of figures, may be misread, but two concluding examples of the most common sort must be allowed to suffice. Look at Figure 3.16 overleaf.

In the case of the upper diagram you will note that the bars of the graph are not continuous, but are interrupted. This is because the bars have been truncated for values below 2200. Why do you suppose this has been done? Suppose that it had not been done. We should then have either a bar graph that was very tall, shooting off the top of the page, or we should have a smaller, scaled-down version in which the differences at the top of the columns, between the values of 2200 and 2500, were microscopically tiny. The interruption provides a way in which the information is clear and on a suitable scale, but the size of the diagram is not overlarge. But care must be taken in using such a diagram. You must not look at the apparent length of the bars, for example, and say that between 1970 and 1975, the number of motor-boats owned in Scotland *doubled*. This would be to misuse the information.

The graph line in the case of the second diagram continues all the way to the year 2000. How valuable is a graph which deals with something which has not happened yet? Of course, we cannot be sure of this information, which is said to be *extrapolated* or *estimated* from existing knowledge. In other words, it is an intelligent guess to think that this is the way that the world's population will move between now and the end of the century. You will note that

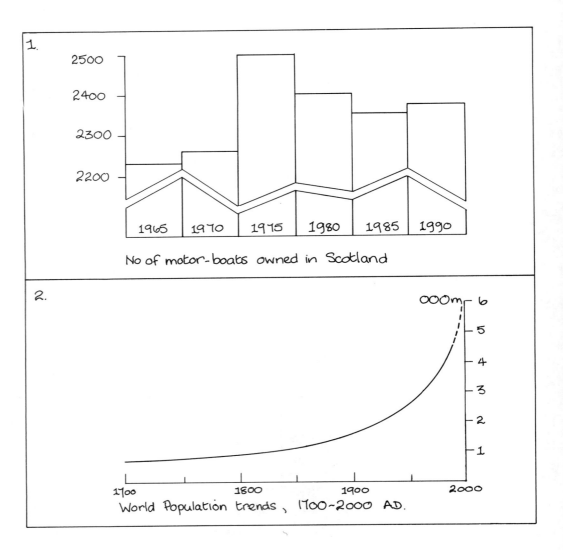

Fig. 3.16 Graphs and diagrams – example (2)

the line of the graph follows a parabolic curve, and that it forms something rather more than a blind guess, since this would seem, mathematically, to be its most likely course. The numbers given on the upright axis in this graph, you will see, are expressed '000m.', or 'thousand million'. The final quantity is 6 000m., or 6 000 000 000. Very often today, according to American usage, this figure is called 'six billion'.

Just as your teachers may prefer you to draw your own map instead of copying someone else's, they may say they prefer you to produce your own statistical data. This is, of course, far from easy. You cannot conjure figures out of thin air; if they are to be reliable figures, they are bound to be taken from a reliable source. But you can usefully make them your own by expressing them in your own way.

a) You can *edit* the figures in order to produce a table substantially different from the one from which you took the information, so that though the work is not completely yours, you can say that you have worked at the information and shaped it to your own requirements.

b) You can *combine* different sorts of figures (where this is possible) from different sources to give a new presentation to your material, perhaps highlighting figures that would not otherwise have been made clear. The figures are not exactly yours, but you are making a new use of them.

c) You can *translate* your information from one statistical form into another. If you have a table you can make it into a graph, pie chart or bar chart (or vice-versa). This will not be new information, but the information at least will have a different appearance. However you handle your figures, you must make your own personal contribution to the work. This is much to be preferred to mechanical copying from one page to another, and then claiming the result as your own.

Footnote
As your work should be indexed and provided with a bibliography, your illustrations should also be listed. It may be better to mount them on separate pieces of paper so that you can adjust their positioning in the assignment if this is required.

PREPARING AND WRITING COURSEWORK ASSIGNMENTS

> **UNIT 1** PRESENTING AN ASSIGNMENT

We will now trace the stages involved in successfully completing one or two pieces of coursework for GCSE History. Firstly, let us take the following assignment:

I To submit a piece of work consisting of several shorter exercises on the Arab-Israeli conflict, 1948–78.

   i) Explain the main causes of the wars between the Israelis and the Arabs in each of the following years: 1948; 1956; 1967; 1972.
   ii) Why did Israel emerge victorious at the end of each of these wars?
   iii) Show how these wars were of major international importance, and involved the interests of the superpowers.
   iv) Explain why some Jewish and Arab leaders were pressing for a peace settlement in 1978, and show how and why their hopes were dashed.

Three of these exercises are *analytical*, and the fourth *empathetic*. The skills to be tested in the first exercise are mainly those relating to *cause*, while *consequence* comes into the second and third exercises. Exercise iii) also requires an evaluation of importance, and of the involvement of the great powers. The last exercise attempts to probe the feelings of some Jewish and Arab leaders in 1978, and deals also with the non-fulfilment of their hopes.

The length of the assignment does not appear to be specified. If, however, we allow 400 words for each part, this will produce a total of 1600 words, which will probably be sufficient for the whole exercise.

> 66 **An analytical assignment** 99

1.1 Planning

You will need to do some background reading before you can effectively tackle any of the parts of this assignment. An outline coverage of the whole question may be obtained by a careful reading of:

   Rayner & Stapley *GCSE World History* (Longman Revise Guide, 1988), Chapter 16

Three other useful outline sources might be found in

Kohler & Taylor, *Africa and the Middle East* (Arnold, *History of the Twentieth Century World Series,* 1985), Chapter 10
E. G. Rayner, *International Affairs* (Arnold, *History of the Twentieth Century World Series,* 1985), Chapter 12
   R. N. Rundle, *International Affairs, 1939–79* (Hodder & Stoughton, 1981)
   Jack Watson, *Twentieth-Century World Affairs* (Murray, Third Edition, 1984), Unit 19

A shorter, more specialised, book (though somewhat older), which has good maps and photographs, and a selection of apt quotations which you may wish to draw on, is

   Bill Mandle, *Conflict in the Promised Land* (Heinemann Educational, 1976)

Many more, and longer, documents (which you may want to look at, although it is less likely that you will want to use them) are to be found in

   Laquer & Rubin, *The Israeli-Arab Reader: A Documentary History of the Middle East Conflict* (Penguin, Fourth Edition, 1984)

You could profitably begin by borrowing these books, or by reading and taking notes from them if you have to consult them in the classroom or the library. Remember that the focus of your interest should be on

- the causes of the wars
- the reasons for the Israeli successes
- the international importance of the wars and the involvement of the superpowers.

If you group your notes on these features you will not drift too far away from the subjects you are intended to cover.

1.2 Preparation

From the Longman Revise Guide (*GCSE World History*), for example, you will get a good idea of the background to the first Arab-Israeli War in 1948. It would clearly be going too far back to mention the Jewish land settlements before the First World War, or even the Balfour Declaration – however important this may have been at the time – since what you are going to write will be limited to about 100 words. Even if you argue that by reason of the importance of the first war in relation to the others you ought to write rather more, you will still not be writing much more than 140 words.

What becomes obvious from the chapter is the continuing problem of Jewish immigration into Israel in the inter-war years, and the increasing friction brought about by Jewish purchases of Palestinian land under the mandate, both of which the British government failed to check. Added to these there was the growing tendency towards terrorism in factions of both communities, leading to renewed violence after the Second World War. The US government was by now throwing its weight behind the Jews, and this encouraged them further. Britain eventually decided to hand over the whole Palestine question to the UN, and announced its intention of pulling out in 1948. The UN Commission on Palestine produced a partition plan for the country into Arab and Jewish zones so similar to an earlier British plan as to suggest that it was copied from it. Neither community was satisfied with this plan, and conflict broke out between them immediately after the British withdrawal.

What you have to do here is to write a passage of about 100 words, focusing your paragraph on the *causes* of the war between the Jews and the Arabs. Some of the graphic details, such as the bomb outrage at the King David Hotel in 1946 which killed 91 British servicemen, or the brutal refusal of entry to over 4500 Jewish illegal immigrants in the appropriately-named *Exodus* at about the same time, will have to be omitted, and what you write must bear directly on the question.

> In the twenty years to 1939 there was a rising tide of Jewish immigration into Palestine, coupled with extensive Jewish purchases of Palestinian land for their farm settlements. By 1942 the Jewish population of the country, at 600,000, actually surpassed the Palestinian Arab population. Arab resentment showed itself in increasing violence. The Jews countered this by the formation of an unofficial Jewish Defence Force known as the Haganah, with its more violent offshoots such as the Irgun Zwei Leumi and the Stern Gang. This terrorism induced Britain to hand over the problem of Palestine to the United Nations. A special Commission on Palestine arranged a partition of the country between the Arabs and the Jews, but this solution was acceptable to neither side, and when British troops withdrew in 1948 war between them broke out. Within hours the infant state of Israel was recognised by the USA and accepted by the General Assembly of UNO.

This is still largely a narrative treatment of the problem, perhaps insufficiently focused on the *causes* of the war. Something more specific ought to be inserted to deal with these causes:

> . . . Palestinian Arab population. The Arabs felt that the Jews had no right to come uninvited into their country and buy up its lands. Their resentment showed itself in frequent resorts to violence . . .

Jewish motivation could also be made more clear:

> . . . and the Stern Gang. The Jews were anxious to escape from persecution and extermination in Europe, and regarded Palestine as their Promised Land. Terrorism on both sides induced Britain . . .

This passage is now however nearer to 200 words than 100, and needs to be carefully pruned. This involves taking out unnecessary words and removing some of the narrative elements in the later part of the paragraph. Some sentences – like the second one – can be removed altogether. The final version will read something like this:

> Before 1939, Jewish immigration and land purchase caused serious problems in Palestine. The Arabs felt that the Jews had no right to come uninvited into their country and buy up its lands. Their resentment showed itself in frequent violence, and the Jews responded equally violently. They were anxious to escape from the Holocaust in Europe, and regarded Palestine as their Promised Land. This terrorism induced Britain to hand over the Palestine problem to the UN, but neither side was satisfied with the partition plan which was produced. When British troops withdrew in 1948 war between the two broke out.

To make it quite clear to which portion of the assignment this answer relates, it is necessary to preface it with a clear indication: (i) (a) 1948.

In preparing an answer to (i) (b), you should take care not to become involved in a detailed account of how Colonel Nasser came to power in Egypt on the overthrow of King Farouk, nor in a complete summary of the policies which led him to undertake the building of the Aswan High Dam and drove him to nationalize the Suez Canal. With only 100 words to hand, it is important to stick to essentials.

> i) b) 1956. Arab states refused to recognise Israel after 1949 and their leader, Colonel Nasser of Egypt, aimed to destroy the new country. Israel was harassed by terrorist attacks, and Israeli shipping was denied the use of the Suez Canal. The Israelis felt sufficiently threatened in 1956 to ally with Britain and France, at that time quarrelling with Egypt over the ownership of the Canal. When the crisis broke, Israeli forces occupied Sinai as far as the Canal, supposedly to safeguard it.

Note also that the question deals with *causes*; you are not expected to go on to a detailed account of the Suez war. Any development of the superpower theme ought to be placed under section (iii).

The same constraints of space apply to your answer to (i) (c). A detailed factual summary of Arab-Israeli relations during the intervening years, 1956–1967, is clearly out of the question, though you may find room for a short quotation to illustrate the feelings existing at the time. You might use one of the quotations on page 32 of Bill Mandle's book *Conflict in the Promised Land*, for example. Your paragraph might run along the following lines:

> i) c) 1967. Arab hostility towards Israel continued to mount in the years before 1967. Egypt and the other Arab states began to rearm with the latest military equipment, and a constant flood of propaganda flowed out from Arab sources. President Aref of Iraq threatened:
>
> > 'The existence of Israel is an error which must be rectified. This is our opportunity to wipe out the ignominy which has been with us since 1948. Our goal is clear – to wipe Israel off the map.'
>
> In 1967 Nasser ordered UN forces out of Sharm-el-Sheikh, and imposed a new blockade on Israeli shipping using the Gulf of Aqaba . . .

The paragraph should then conclude with a reference to the Israeli reaction to the Arab attitude. The Israeli government, rather than sit motionless awaiting what it saw as the inevitable decision, decided to get its blow in first with an attack designed to forestall the Arab attack:

> . . . The Israelis, thoroughly frightened, but with their armed forces newly reshaped, decided on a bold pre-emptive strike to deal with the country's enemies.

Taking the quotation into account, this paragraph is rather longer than it should be. However, since both (a) and (b) are a little shorter, you have a little space in hand. What you must avoid is getting involved in the dramatic narrative details of the actual conduct of the war.

Events did not stand still between 1967 and 1973, and you must make an attempt to deal briefly with them in your answer to (i) (d).

> i) d) 1973. Outrages by Arab terrorist organizations such as the PLO, and a spate of aircraft hijackings to keep the issue in the public eye, developed after the Six Days' War. The most serious of these occurred at Lydda airport in 1972, and later at the Munich Olympic Games. Between Israel and the Arab Powers there was a state of uneasy peace. Terrorism occurred frequently and the PLO maintained a state of undeclared war. There was also an Arab-operated price-ring for petrol (OPEC) to bring pressure on Western states to limit their support for Israel. Egypt and Syria had once again equipped themselves with Soviet arms. Acting more stealthily this time, they launched their attack in 1973 at the time of the Yom Kippur festival, when many Jews were in their synagogues.

1.3 Completing the writing

The answers to part (ii) of this assignment will be similarly sub-divided. You will notice that the requirement to explain Israel's victory 'at the end of *each* of these wars' means that you cannot lump the reasons for Israel's survival together and deal with them all at once. Of course, some of these reasons will be the same in each case, and you will have to find some way of dealing with this problem without too much repetition of the same material. A little thought will show you how to do it effectively.

> ii) The surrounding Arab states of Iraq, Jordan, Syria and Egypt did not always act together – as in 1973 when both Iraq and Jordan remained neutral. They were also generally poorly prepared for conflict and lacked a unified higher military command. Israel, on the other hand, showed great resolution and was fighting for its very existence. Israel enjoyed considerable support from abroad, and also had the advantage of interior lines of communication and often the very latest military equipment and expertise.
> a) In 1948 Israel was determined to act swiftly to secure its independence, and Ben Gurion promptly proclaimed the existence of the state of Israel on the day the British left. The Jewish immigrants, many of them newly arrived from Europe and with the memories of the concentration camps still fresh in their minds, were ready to lay their lives on the line for their new state. Though they had some difficult moments in the early stages of the war, their determination paid off and their Arab neighbours had to ask for armistices.
> b) In 1956 it is arguable whether Israel eventually emerged 'victorious'. The Jews were certainly able to overrun Sinai for a time, but political reasons forced them to retire from the occupied territories at the end of the war, and for some years an uneasy peace resulted along the Gaza-Eilat armistice line. The war, however, provided proof of Israel's continuing patriotic zeal, and of its capacity to win and to survive.
> c) During the Six Days War in 1967 it was the speed and tactical superiority of the Israelis that overwhelmed the Arabs. Within hours, the Egyptian airforce was destroyed on the ground, and inside three days Jewish forces were on the east bank of the Canal once more. Despite all their claims, Israel's Arab enemies were ill-prepared and easily out-manoeuvred, while the Jews were buoyed up by the grit and determination of their War Minister, Moshe Dayan.
> d) Though taken by surprise in 1973, Israeli forces soon astonished the world by recovering the initiative. They destroyed over 1000 Syrian tanks in the Golan Heights, cut off the entire Egyptian Third Army in a huge pocket west of the Canal, and crossed the Canal to take the port of Suez in the rear. The neutrality of Jordan weakened the Arabs' efforts, while the USA and the USSR joined to arrange a cease-fire and end the war. Military discipline and a strong sense of national unity had enabled the new state to survive.

In part (iii) of this question it is possible to discuss the wars together rather than separately. In this section, the focus of your answer has to be on *international importance* and *the interests of the superpowers*.

> iii) As colonialism in the Near East wound down at the end of the Second World War and the British and French mandates ended, national, religious and cultural differences within the area began to re-emerge. The countries of the Arab world, scattered from Morocco to the Persian Gulf and including many of the rich oil states of the Middle East, joined in condemnation of Israel and later began to use OPEC to bring pressure to bear on the oil-importing nations to stop supporting Israel. The Jews, for their part, scattered widely throughout the world as a result of the *diaspora*, employed a powerful

lobby in Washington and brought pressure to bear in several other Western countries to rally diplomatic, financial and military support for their cause. They also played on the guilt feelings arising out of the wartime Holocaust on the part of the European governments such as West Germany. Both Jews and Arabs tried to use the public forum of the UN as a means of influencing world opinion on their behalf. Unofficially, too, the activities of terrorist groups such as the PFLP and Black September aroused much international concern, just as did various aircraft hijackings, and there was a consequent tightening of police supervision and airport security. Britain tried to be even-handed in its dealings with the two sides, but other countries such as France openly favoured Israel and supplied it lavishly with arms. At the same time, the PLO spread Arab extremism widely in the Mediterranean area, fostering disruptive activities close to Israel in Jordan and the Lebanon. They also transferred their headquarters to Tunisia in 1983, and encouraged the growth of other extremist policies e.g. those of Moammur Ghaddafi in Libya.

The superpowers also found themselves enmeshed in the Near East. The USA had a very powerful Jewish community which influenced successive American governments and brought pressure to bear at presidential election times. Washington had strategic interests in the Persian Gulf, and remained a major importer of Middle Eastern oil; they also resented Soviet attempts to treat the Near East as their own 'back yard', and denounced the Russian encouragement of nationalist regimes in countries such as Syria. The USSR, for its part, rejected US meddling in the region, favouring the Arabs instead of the Israelis. Soviet leaders had sound strategic and ideological reasons for opposing western colonialism, and supporting friendly governments in the area. Thus the USSR supported the Arab governments and supplied them with arms and encouragement, just as the USA supported Israel. They agreed in condemning Anglo-French adventurism in Egypt at the time of the Suez crisis in 1956, but in most other cases took opposite sides.

The empathetic slant of part (iv) of this question requires you to put yourself in the shoes of the Jewish and Arab leaders mentioned, though the last part of this sub-question is more analytical than empathetic, requiring some attention to both *how* and *why*.

iv) Many Jewish leaders in 1978 – even the Prime Minister Menachem Begin (himself a former leader of the Stern Gang) – had come to favour a peace settlement with their Arab foes. The wars had imposed a heavy toll of casualties, and the strain on the economy had been severe. In 1974 Israel had been forced to devalue the currency by 43%, and there was an inflation rate of nearly 100% per annum. Israeli leaders were sensitive to international criticism of the behaviour of their military units, and regretted the air of perpetual crisis in which their young people were forced to live. The accession to power in Egypt of the moderate Anwar Sadat on the death of Nasser in 1970 and the dwindling enthusiasm of Hussein of Jordan for the Arab cause provided the Israelis with an opportunity of dividing the opposition and achieving a degree of security after over thirty years of conflict.

Moderate opinion in Egypt favoured a settlement with Israel for similar reasons. The peace proposals put forward in 1978 at the time of the Camp David Agreement offered Egypt much of what the country needed to salve its wounded feelings – the evacuation of Israeli-occupied Egyptian territory and promises of Israeli concessions in return for diplomatic recognition. The activities of extremists had earned the Arab national movement a bad name, and the further continuance of the war seemed futile and costly. Loss of trade, inflation, high taxes and government debt, the heavy cost of armaments and continuing national poverty all tended to show the wisdom of agreeing terms with the Israelis and ending thirty years of conflict. Already the extremists had procured the death of President Sadat, but his successor, Hosni Mubarak, pressed on with the achievement of peace.

In accordance with the terms agreed, Israel carried out the evacuation of the Sinai Peninsula in three stages in the early 1980s, but thereafter the peace process broke down. The Israeli government in 1980 transferred the capital to Jerusalem, whose Israeli ownership the Arab states disputed, and carried on with its policy of planting new settlements on the West Bank. Israeli garrisons continued to mistreat the inmates of refugee camps in Gaza and elsewhere, and reacted harshly to Palestinian protests against their presence. The Golan Heights were also formally annexed from Syria, and Israeli garrisons in southern Lebanon were reinforced. For their part, Arab radicals continued to think it was little more than a capitulation to accept a negotiated peace. They pointed to violations as evidence of Israeli bad faith, and asserted that non-fulfilment of the peace conditions meant that war between the two sides was still continuing.

1.4 Examiner's mark scheme

How well did we do?

On an assignment of this kind, the examiner will set out his mark scheme in the form of the various *levels of achievement*. There may be anything up to four or five of these different levels, but in many cases the levels will be *three* in number, and the marks awarded accordingly.

i) **Target:** *To outline the causes of the Arab-Israeli wars of 1948–49, 1956, 1967 and 1973*

Level 1	Scattered narrative of some of the developments	*1–5 marks*
Level 2	General narrative from which some elementary analysis emerges	*6–12 marks*
Level 3	Good analysis based on effective selection of evidence	*13–20 marks*

ii) **Target:** *Explaining the reasons for Israel's success in each of the wars*

Level 1	Narrative of some of the wars	*1–3 marks*
Level 2	Some elementary reasons for Israeli success in individual wars or uneven analysis of both international and superpower aspects	*4–6 marks*
Level 3	Thorough analysis of reasons for Israeli success in each of the wars	*7–10 marks*

iii) **Target:** *Assessing the international importance of the wars and the extent of the involvement of the superpowers*

Level 1	Individual mentions of actions of outside powers	*1–3 marks*
Level 2	Some analysis with attention to *either* international importance *or* superpower involvement	*4–6 marks*
Level 3	Thorough analysis of both aspects required	*7–10 marks*

iv) **Target:** *Explaining the support of Jewish and Arab leaders for peace in 1978 and explaining how and why they were disappointed*

Level 1	Narrative of peace moves and statement of failure	*1–3 marks*
Level 2	Reasons for peace moves with a little empathetic understanding of one side or the other; explanation of failure	*4–6 marks*
Level 3	Reasons for peace moves with some empathetic understanding of one side or the other; explanation of failure	*6–7 marks*
Level 4	Good empathetic understanding of wishes for peace by moderates on both sides, and *how* and *why* of disappointment	*8–10 marks*

Try to work out for yourself how highly the answers drafted above would have scored under this mark scheme. You ought to find that the answers reach to Levels 3 or 4 in each case – can you see why?

UNIT 2 PRESENTING A SECOND ASSIGNMENT

A documentary assignment

Now let us take a look at an assignment based on the comparative evaluation of historical evidence. You will see that this time the various sub-questions are provided with mark tariffs. The initial identification part scores the least, since presumably every candidate is expected to be able to deduce that the whole assignment is on the subject of race relations. The next four sub-questions, (b) to (e), score relatively more heavily, and each is based on one of the pieces of evidence. Part (f) is weighted the most heavily, since this is the part that deals with the comparative evaluation of the evidence.

II Study the two cartoons and the two extracts, and then answer questions (a) to (f) which follow.

Cartoon A (from the *Observer*, June 1965).

'You people lower the tone of the locality.'

Cartoon B (from the *Sunday Express*, July 1967).

Extract A (from a leading article in *The Times*, 6 July 1968).

The Tories and Race

line 1   Is it fair to charge the Conservatives who are threatening to oppose the Race Relations Bill on the third Reading with prejudice? Those who know the atmosphere of the Conservative Party and the frame of mind of that group cannot really doubt that most of them are prejudiced. Mr Enoch Powell's is an extreme example of their attitude and his
line 5   speech and his subsequent references to the subject have all shown the same fear of coloured people, an irrational fear which is the mother of prejudice itself. As one reads through the list of Conservative members who are preparing to oppose the Bill, one must ask how many are really free of this fear, how many really believe that opposition to the Bill is a natural expression of the brotherhood of man.
line 10   Of course, it is wrong to condemn them as wicked men, though they may be men whose ideas would have wicked consequences, yet they represent a stifling narrowing of the Conservative tradition . . . Theirs is the stifling Conservatism of . . . small gains, small hopes, and fear your neighbour as yourself.

Extract B   (from a letter in the correspondence columns of *The Times*, 9 July 1968).

Sir: In your article entitled 'The Tories and Race' (July 6) you made a most unfair attack
line 15   upon the Conservative MPs who intended to vote against the third Reading of the Race Relations Bill. You suggest that they are inspired by racial prejudice and 'do not care how their fellow citizens are treated'.
    When the Conservative Party voted against the Bill on the second Reading the reasons were set out clearly in an Opposition motion moved by Mr. Quintin Hogg in the
line 20   following terms:
    'That this House, reaffirming its condemnation of racial discrimination and accepting the need for steps designed to improve the situation, nevertheless declines to give a second Reading to a Bill which, on balance, will not in its practical application contribute to the achievement of racial harmony.'
        . . . Yours faithfully,
line 25   Duncan Sandys
    (House of Commons, July 6)

a) To what political problem do both the cartoons and both the extracts refer?   *(1)*
b) In the case of Cartoon A:
   i) suggest the area of the world the man on the doorstep had come from, together with a possible reason why he had come to Britain; and
   ii) explain the irony of the caption to the cartoon.   *(4)*
c) In the case of Cartoon B:
   i) identify the figures in the upper and lower windows of the house; and
   ii) explain what the cartoonist is implying by the words shown pinned up on the large notice on the door.   *(4)*
d) What criticisms are suggested in Extract A of *Conservatives* who were *threatening to oppose the Race Relations Bill* (lines 1–2)?   *(3)*
e) How effectively does the letter from Duncan Sandys answer the criticisms made of the Conservative *opposition* (line 21) to this Bill?   *(3)*
f) With which of the extracts is Cartoon A in broad agreement, and with which is Cartoon B in agreement? Give reasons for your choice.   *(10)*

2.1 Planning and preparation

The instruction to *study the evidence* at the start of the assignment means that you must spend some time examining it before attempting any of the questions.

Let us take Cartoon A. The woman standing in the open doorway of the house in the cartoon appears to be a boarding-house landlady, and the sentence forming the caption is the remark she is making to the black man on her doorstep. The bag he is carrying suggests he has just arrived, and her general attitude seems to be one of disapproval of him – perhaps to the point of not accepting him as a lodger. There are four rather peculiar figures in the street. All of them are wearing hats, and carrying briefcases and umbrellas. They are swathed in some sort of white material, but they cannot be ghosts. Two of them are carrying large wooden crosses over their shoulders. It seems likely that the sheets are intended as a sort of disguise, with slits cut for the eyes – the most sensible suggestion is that they are intended to be members of the Ku Klux Klan, the racially-motivated group which often victimises negroes in the Deep South of the USA. The implication is that the landlady thinks it is discreditable to take a coloured lodger, but sees nothing shameful in permitting those in the area to parade their racial prejudices.

The house in Cartoon B seems to symbolise Britain, judging by the union flag which is flying from the chimney. The house appears to be well equipped to deal with the danger of fire, for there is a very substantial fire-hose with a large nozzle on the outside wall, and a water

CHAPTER 4 **PRESENTING A SECOND ASSIGNMENT** 53

hydrant nearby. Nevertheless, the garage of the house seems to be on fire, the black smoke is being made out to represent the danger of British racism. The occupant, however, is sound asleep in his front room, his hands comfortably folded across his middle and looking very satisfied with himself. The notice on the front door reveals his identity, and suggests he will be none too pleased to be roused from his slumbers.

Similar detailed attention must be given to the two extracts. They must be carefully read and understood, and any difficult words such as *stifling* or *reaffirming* looked up. You will also have to understand what is meant by the *second* or the *third readings* of parliamentary *Bills*. If the sentences are long or complicated, you must attempt to unravel them, so you know exactly what each extract means. Extract B was written only a few days after Extract A, and you must understand how the writer of the letter, a Conservative MP, intends it to be a reply to the leading article in *The Times*.

Next you must study the sub-questions and the mark tariff allowed for each. Only a short answer will be needed for (a), which has a mark allocation of 1 out of 25. More thought is needed for the comprehension elements in (b) and (c), both of which are sub-divided into two parts, with something like 2 marks awarded for each of (i) and (ii) in both cases. Sections (d) and (e) invite you to interpret the meanings of the two extracts, for a reward of 3 marks in each case. It is the final analytic and evaluative sub-question, (f), with 10 marks out of 25, which requires the exercise of the highest abilities, and which demands the most detailed attention and the fullest treatment. In answering all these sub-questions particular care must be taken not to duplicate or to overlap the answer material, so that your answers will not be repetitive.

2.2 Completing the writing

All the pieces of evidence have to do with matters of *race* or *colour*. The cartoons seem to be dealing with the question of coloured *immigration*, judging by the colour of the man on the doorstep in Cartoon A, and by the phrase on the nozzle of the hosepipe in Cartoon B. The extracts seem to be dealing with the question of *race relations*. You have to be careful that the answer you give relates to *both* the extracts and the cartoons. It could also usefully be employed to provide an indication of the period to which the evidence relates.

a) The racial problem in Britain in the 1960s.

The first part of (b) leaves you with some flexibility, since any place from which there was immigration in the 1960s ought to be acceptable. You should note, however, that if you are to remain true to the spirit of the cartoon, you ought to be speaking of negro immigration rather than Asian. There were, of course, problems arising out of Kenyan immigration later in the 1960s, but the context of this cartoon seems to be plainly West Indian. The reasons for this immigration concerned the high level of unemployment then prevailing in the West Indian countries.

Part (ii) is perhaps not quite so straightforward. For one thing, you will have to understand what the question means by the word *irony*. Irony consists of saying the opposite of what is meant in a way that will make the underlying meaning clear, or, more subtly (as in this case), having an underlying meaning that is quite different from the obvious meaning on the surface. Thus, when a landlady refuses to take a lodger on the ground that this might be letting down the tone of the neighbourhood, she has to be sure that there are not others nearby who are already letting down the neighbourhood much more drastically.

b)	i) The negro immigrant has probably come to Britain from Jamaica or Trinidad. Many West Indians came to Britain at this time because of the poverty in their own countries, and this one was probably going to take a job as a bus driver or as a mortuary attendant.
	ii) The boarding-house landlady seems indignant, and according to the caption she is saying that to take a coloured boarder would 'lower the tone' of the neighbourhood. The irony is that she seems to be unaware that the atmosphere of the 'locality' is already rather unsavoury, since it appears to be frequented by the people portrayed by the cartoonist as Ku Klux Klan members, i.e. people violently prejudiced against the blacks.

Sub-question (c) is also divided into two parts, the first of which, again, is easier than the second. Part (i) asks for two identifications. In the lower window is a sleeping figure named on the notice alongside as 'Mr Wilson'. This may have to suffice for an answer, if you are unaware who Mr Wilson is, but if from your knowledge of the 1960s you are able to identify him as the Prime Minister at that time, it would be helpful to say so. There is a female in the upstairs window who looks distinctly alarmed; she is wearing a crested helmet and is carrying a trident – probably a pointer to her identity. If you still do not know who she is, observe the flag on the chimney and note that the house is intended to be Britain. Who might this occupant be? You ought to note carefully, too, that in making these identifications, you ought to take care to say *which is which*, or, at least, to get your answers in the same order as is requested in the question; if you do not, the examiner may misunderstand your answer.

The notice referred to in part (ii) seems to be critical of the self-satisfied Mr Wilson, snugly sleeping while his house is burning. The cartoonist implies that a cry of 'Fire!', though unpopular, would be useful, and that it would be much more sensible if Mr Wilson were to get the hosepipe and quench the flames. You must take care to link your answer to the theme of 'racial prejudice' which is indicated in the dense cloud of smoke coming from the burning garage, and mentioned in the notice pinned on the front door.

> c) i) The figure in the upper window seems to be Britannia in her traditional costume, and the figure in the lower window is Mr Harold Wilson, the Labour Prime Minister at that time.
>   ii) The cartoonist is suggesting that the smug Mr Wilson is carelessly sleeping while his house is burning, and according to the notice on the door would not take kindly to being awakened from his slumbers. He presumably does not care enough about the racial problem to want to be troubled with it. The cartoonist implies that it would be much more sensible to deal with the problem, e.g. by using the hose-reel conveniently situated alongside his house to quench the fires likely to result from unrestricted coloured immigration.

In order to find out the answer to (d) you have to read through Extract A once again to find the criticisms of the Conservatives who were opponents of the Race Relations Bill of 1968. There is a clear indication of the leader-writer's opinion in the second sentence that they were *prejudiced*; a criticism that is borne out in the remainder of the first paragraph by references to their *irrational fear* and their insufficient regard for the *brotherhood of man*. In the second paragraph the objectors are said to be doing serious damage to the *Conservative tradition* by associating it with rigidity and small-mindedness. The concluding phrase, 'Fear your neighbour as yourself' is an ironic echo of the Christian doctrine of 'Love your neighbour as yourself'.

> d) There are two main criticisms in Extract A. The writer of the leader says that most of the Conservatives who oppose the Race Relations Bill are racially prejudiced, and, like Enoch Powell (who is often alleged to be racist in his attitudes), show an irrational fear of coloured people. They seem to be unaware that their racist fears are incompatible with the idea of the 'brotherhood of man'. Further, in the second paragraph, the leader-writer goes on to say that their narrowness and small-mindedness are quite foreign to the tolerant and generous tradition of British Conservatism. The final phrase 'Fear your neighbour as yourself' (instead of 'Love your neighbour') carries the implication that racism is also quite unchristian.

The letter to the Editor of *The Times* from which Extract B is taken attempts to answer these criticisms. In doing so, it justifies the Conservative rejection of the criticisms by quoting the terms of the Amendment which Conservatives proposed at the time of their opposition to the Bill. The question asks *how effectively* this letter answers the criticisms made of Conservative opposition to the Bill. The letter must be carefully re-read with this question in mind.

> e) Extract B seems a rather ingenious and in some ways quite an effective answer to the criticisms made of the Conservatives for their earlier opposition to the Bill. In the letter Mr Sandys says that the leader-writer is quite wrong to think that Conservatives who opposed the third reading of the Race Relations Bill were motivated by racial prejudice. It is also untrue to suggest that they 'do not care how their fellow citizens are treated'. He points to the actual terms of the Amendment they moved in order to give what he says is the real reason for their opposition. This amendment in fact condemns racial discrimination and suggests that action ought to be taken to improve the situation, but it makes the particular point that the Bill under discussion was unlikely to do this. It is the likely ineffectiveness of the Bill rather than its condemnation of racial prejudice which leaves its Conservative critics dissatisfied. At the same time Sandys was perhaps wise in his letter to ignore the reference made in the leader article to Enoch Powell, rather than to try to distance his party from Powell. In fact, Powell's views were not without support, and to have admitted this honestly would have weakened Sandys's case.

You must take care in preparing your answer to the final sub-question that you have thoroughly understood the meanings of the four pieces of evidence. You should also be sure that what you write in your answer is sufficient to earn you the full 10 marks allowed.

> f) Cartoon A takes an unfavourable view of the white residents of the area in question, and suggests both that the landlady is herself racially prejudiced, and that she is doing a disservice to the black man who is seeking accommodation. The cartoonist also regards racially-inspired movements such as the Ku Klux Klan in an unfavourable light, and thinks they are a much more serious danger than the colour problem they are designed to remedy. The cartoonist's attitude may be said to be high-minded and disinterested.
>
> Cartoon B expresses disapproval for the sluggishness and neglect of the Prime Minister in allowing the country to suffer from the problems resulting from black immigration when he could so easily find the right remedy. The cartoonist believes that the 'British race problem' is spreading like a fire, but that a ban on immigration would provide a swift and effective way of dealing with it. The cartoon does not express any uncharitable views of coloured people, but in demanding prompt action to check immigration seems to suggest that a dangerous problem exists which demands a prompt solution.
>
> Extract A, though with apparent reluctance, charges the Conservative opponents of the Race Relations Bill with racial prejudice, and says that what they are doing is likely to give British Conservatives a bad name. It takes the view that, however innocently, they are embarking on a course of action that may have evil consequences. The tone of the extract is hostile to 'stifling narrowness', and is generally magnanimous and philosophical.
>
> Extract B rejects this criticism, and claims that the opponents of the Bill are not motivated by racial prejudice, and that they care as much as anyone else about their fellow citizens. The real reason for their opposition to the Bill is that they do not think it will prove effective in achieving the harmony it is seeking to bring about. They are not impressed by these proposals, and think there are more effective ways of solving the race problem than the one put forward by the government. The opponents of the Bill deny any suggestion of prejudice, but think that race relations consitute a real problem.
>
> Cartoon A and Extract A, by their tone of philosophical high-mindedness, seem to have a lot in common. They concern themselves very little with the practical day-to-day problems arising in communities of mixed race, and both carry the unspoken implication that the real trouble stems not from the coloured people, but from their white counterparts, some of whom may not even be aware how prejudiced they are. Cartoon B and Extract B, on the other hand, admit that a real problem exists and that all right-thinking people should be aware of it and should be willing to take appropriate measures to deal with it. At the same time they both suggest that the attitudes currently being adopted by the government are regrettable. They suggest, however, that the problem is an urgent one, and that delay is ill-advised.

2.3 Examiner's mark scheme

> **How well did we do?**

This exercise incorporates an *incline of difficulty*, i.e. the easy earlier parts lead up to more difficult parts, demanding a higher order of skills. Thus, identification of the subject-area of the assignment scores only 1 mark, comprehension of various features of the evidence scores 3 or 4 marks in each case, and the final comparative evaluation and comparison of the evidence 10 marks.

Target: *Comprehension, evaluation and comparison of sources*

a) Race/race relations/racial discrimination. To gain credit, the political problem must apply to all four pieces of evidence.   *1 mark*

b) 2 + 2 marks
  i) The West Indies/British West Indies. The name(s) of any West Indian territory should also be accepted, if appropriately given.   *1 mark*
  To take up some unskilled or semi-skilled employment   *1 mark*
  ii) Simple paraphrase of meaning of cartoon   *1 mark*
  Better answers indicating *irony*   *1 further mark*

c) 2 + 2 marks
  i) Britannia, upper window; Mr Wilson (or Prime Minister), lower window   *1 mark for each identification*
  ii) Simple paraphrase of meaning of notice   *1 mark*
  Better answers indicating *comprehension*   *1 further mark*

d) Level 1: Paraphrase of article — *1 mark*
   Level 2: Answer from which criticism and some explanation emerges — *2 marks*
   Level 3: Good explanation based on well-observed criticisms — *3 marks*

e) Level 1: Paraphrase of letter — *1 mark*
   Level 2: Answer identifying difference and offering some explanation — *2 marks*
   Level 3: Well-observed differences with convincing explanations — *3 marks*

f) Level 1: Simple comprehension and explanation of any piece of evidence, 1 mark each, up to 3 — *1–3 marks*
   Level 2: Explanation and evaluation of any piece of evidence, 1 mark each, up to 3 — *4–6 marks*
   Level 3: Effective comparison, with well-supported conclusion — *7–10 marks*

Answers close to the one offered in this chapter ought to score very highly, coming well within the range of a Grade A.

2.4 Sources

We acknowledge the following sources which were used in compiling question II:

Cartoon A *Observer*, 13 June 1965.
Cartoon B *Sunday Express*, 9 July 1967.
   Both these cartoons are reprinted on pp. 174 and 175 of *Daily Sketches*, ed. Martin Walker (Paladin, 1978).
Extract A *The Times* first leader, 6 July 1968.
Extract B *The Times* correspondence columns, 9 July 1968.

CHAPTER 5

EXAMPLES OF STUDENTS' COURSEWORK

This chapter contains a number of *actual examples* of pieces of coursework submitted by students. Study each assignment carefully and note the *assessment obective(s)*. Then *read the student answer* and decide whether you think it

> carries out the task set
> meets the assessment objective(s)
> is a good example of what a student ought to be able to do.

❝ Deal with each of these carefully. ❞

Having made up your *own* mind about the quality of the work, compare *your verdict* with that of the *examiner*, given at the end of each example. Congratulate yourself if you and the examiner are in general agreement; if not, make sure that you understand *why* you differ and see if you can get closer to the examiner's view on the next example.

UNIT 1 EUROPEAN UNITY

Assessment objective 2: cause and consequence.

Why was there a growing body of opinion in Britain supporting the ideal of European unity? Why, nevertheless, in the British referendum of 1975, were 33% of those voting against the idea?

1.1 Student's answer

> There was a lot of difference of opinion in Britain about the EEC during the 1960s and 1970s, with some people in favour of joining and others deeply against it. The divisions were not along party lines. Keen suporters of the European movement included Edward Heath and Harold Macmillan who were Conservatives, and also Lord George Brown who was a member of the Labour Party. The Liberal Party under Jeremy Thorpe was the only British party to make it part of its program. As a result of all these things, the question of joining the EEC was very controversial.
> Soon after the Treaty of Rome, The British government had taken the lead in setting up the European Free Trade Association, or EFTA, as an alternative to the EEC. It had seven members: these were Britain, Denmark, Sweden, Norway, Portugal, Austria and Switzerland. These states agreed to faze out all customs dutys over a ten-year period on a voluntary basis taking account of each country's committments to other nations with which they had agreements e.g. the Empire. But EFTA was never as strong or as succesful as the EEC, nor did the Seven have anything like the same industrial capacity as the European Six.
> So Britain changed direction in the 1960s and made three trys to get into the Common Market. In 1962 and 1967 there efforts were not crowned with success. General de Gaulle spikeheaded the resistance,

> arguing that Britain was too week and trecherous to be allowed to become a member. But in 1970 Edward Heath became the British Prime Minister, and he persuaded the new French President, Pompidou, to allow Britain to enter the Community. So too did Ireland and Denmark; thus the EEC became the 'Nine' instead of the 'Six' and EFTA collapsed.
>
> In 1975 Harold Wilson, now Labour Prime Minister, became an enthusiastic supporter of the EEC. He renegotiated the terms of Britain's entry because he did not like them, and put the issue in front of the British people in the form of a referendum, advising them to make up their own minds and follow the Labour Party's lead in rejecting it. Fortunately the nation was more sensible than Wilson gave them credit for, and voted overwhelmingly in favour of membership of the Common Market.

1.2 Examiner's comments

I wonder if the student who wrote this piece of work noticed that the assessment objective was concerned with cause and consequence? It really is rather difficult to find much cause and consequence here. It concentrates mainly on description, and emphasizes *who* supported the EEC rather than *why* they supported it. Nor is there any attempt to explain why so many people opposed the EEC in the referendum. The lack of argument and focus makes this an unsatisfactory piece of work, made worse by its brevity and lack of accurate data. Furthermore, the student obviously hopes that the examiner will not notice the fact that the work is heavily dependent on one source, R.D.H. Seaman's *Britain and Western Europe* (Arnold, 1983 – see p. 189 onwards). Since the student does *not* acknowledge this source (or, for that matter, any other source) it seems likely that he is trying to conceal the fact that he has lifted much of his material from it. Even this source, as you can see if you compare this work with the original, is not well used: Harold Wilson did not become 'an enthusiastic supporter of the EEC'; nor, on the other hand, did he advise the British people to reject the EEC in the referendum, which would seem to be a contradiction of his alleged enthusiasm. This inaccurate idea of Wilson does less than justice to Wilson's political subtlety over the Common Market issue.

This rather brief piece of coursework could be a lot better presented. It contains unnecessary spelling mistakes, and the writing does not flow very smoothly. As it is so weak overall, the work would be assessed at quite a low mark. It needs depth, accuracy and sharpness of focus. But it does show evidence of a certain maturity of vocabulary and style.

UNIT 2 — CHINESE AND CUBAN REVOLUTIONS

Assessment objective 2: similarity and difference.

> To what extent is it true to suggest that the Chinese revolution of 1949 and the Cuban revolution of 1959 were both brought about by the sufferings of the people and their exploitation by feudal rulers? What differences can you see between the two régimes which the revolutions established?

2.1 Student's answer

> In 1945 the national government of Chiang Kai-shek was a steadily decaying regime, heavily dependent on US assistance for its continued survival. Soon the Communists began a major drive from Manchuria towards the south, Mao said: "Wars are not won by gadgets, but by deddicated men". The Nationalists lacked popular support and soon crumbled; the Communists advanced more quickly than even Mao had dared to hope. The Nationalists were hopelessly currupt and there was massive post-war inflation. Soon in the mountains the Nationalist armies melted away; those who were still loyal to Chiang fled to

Formosa (Taiwan) with him in 1949 and set up a temporary government there. In October Mao proclaimed the People's Republic, saying: "Our nation will never again be an insulted nation. We have stood up."

There was great poverty in China, and the condition of the people was scarely better than the animals in the fields. Babies had their feet bound, and women were bought and sold in hard times. Fuedal Lords, who owned nearly all the land, charged high rents and kept people in conditions of hunger and suffering. There were few towns. These were like the fish that swam in the ocean of the peasantry, and there were often floods which washed away the crops they needed. There were also foreign influences in China which were resented. The Chinese called them the "western barbarians" and were exploited by them. They also worshipped their ansestors.

In Cuba, too, there was great suffering. The weather was hot and there was much poverty and American tourism. The land was owned by big land-owners who's powers over their peasants was great. Landless workers toiled on their lord's estates, and most of the land was in the hands of a small number of fuedal masters. The Catholic Church also had much power. Most of the industries in Cuba were owned by US investors such as the United Fruit Company which did a lot of business in bananas. US companies owned the telephones and the telegraphs, the railways and much of the little industry which the island possessed. It is not surprising that the Cubans hated foreigners almost as much as the Chinese did.

Both new governments in these two countries were communist in inclination. They took over the land, which they divided out afresh between the ordinary peasants, and they nationalized the country's industries and businesses. Both were friendly towards the Soviet Union at least to begin with. But there were important differences. One country was a very large and populus Asian nation, the other quite a small Carribean island. There versions of communism also had important differences. You might say that Chinese communism was rice-flavoured, but Cuban communism was tobacco-flavoured. It was true that both adapted the teachings of communism to suit the local conditions which prevaled in their different countries.

2.2 Examiner's comments

Here a *comparison* is asked for, yet the work begins with a *description*. Only in the line about corruption and inflation does the first paragraph come close to mentioning (though not assessing) corruption and exploitation. This is probably because the student has abandoned the idea of analysis in favour of closely reproducing the text from the beginning of Chapter 10 of the book by John and Gwynneth Stokes *Europe and the Modern World, 1870–1970* (Longman, 1973 – see p. 310. Unfortunately the coverage of this book is not entirely suitable for a topic like this one.) Perhaps the student thought that the examiner was unfamiliar with the standard textbooks and would not notice this heavy dependency. Perhaps he thought, too, that as his analysis was shaky some description of Chinese sufferings was needed after all; so in his second paragraph he provides a harrowing picture. It makes sweeping generalizations more appropriate to China in the mid-nineteenth century than the mid-twentieth. Some attempt should at least have been made to assess the extent to which the customs and conditions described here continued into the 1940s.

The comparison with Cuba is made by placing the descriptions of the two countries consecutively, instead of using the superior method of a *point-by-point* comparison. Cuba's hot weather sounds like an odd sort of suffering! But at the end an effective, though brief, comparison of the two regimes is offered in the final paragraph. This could have been much further developed, but it is a useful model on how to tackle a comparison.

Once again there is no bibliography, and the irritating spelling mistakes continue – these may be forgiveable under examination conditions, but could easily be avoided in prepared work by the simple use of a dictionary. This work is certainly superior in quality to the previous example, but the merit of the last paragraph is not matched in its opening lines. The student should have given more thought to *planning* and to meeting the required assessment objectives.

UNIT 3 INDIA

Assessment objective 2: continuity and change.

How far have the problems of the Indian sub-continent been worsened or alleviated by political independence in 1948?

3.1 Student's answer

India's problems arose from the nature of the country. It was a heavily-populated country, with many different languages and religions. The customs of the country were very difficult. The pig was unclean to the Muslim, and the cow sacred to the Hindu. The country was largely agricultural, with millions of peasant families scratching a miserable living from the soil. Shortage of coal and wood meant that the farmers had to burn their cow dung as fuel for the fires, which otherwise they would have been able to use it to fertilize the land. There was very little industry except what was owned by foreign firms relying on cheap Indian labour, as in the textile mills of Calcutta. Living standards were low, education was bad and the level of public services such as health left much to be desired. The seething millions of the sub-continent were often in ferment, and it was this, rather than any deliberate desire to repress the country which made the British so slow to give independence.

In a way, the granting of independence created problems of its own, and made the situation worse. The problem of carving two Pakistans — East and West — out of India was bloody and painful. There was much inter-communal strife, and many thousands of casualties, especially in the areas where the population was mixed. There were disputes too over canal waters, government debt, the sharing of the Reserve Bank's assets, and of course over the future of Kashmir. Ways had to be found to link the princely states with the new governments. India, too, had to try to operate a democracy with an electorate that was largely illiterate. Poverty, too, still remained, and it was difficult to persuade Indians who had put all the ills of their country down to British misgovernment to accept that independence alone was not the answer to all these problems. Even in foreign policy there were problems. Though large, India was weak; so they tried to make a virtue out of necessity by declaring for a policy of "non-alignment" with the plans of the stronger world powers.

In fact, as far as basic problems went, independence solved nothing. The country was still very poor, heavily dependent on agriculture, short of industrial capital, low on public services, and now it had to fight its problems all alone. The cultural and religious problems of the country still remained — so did the problem of corruption amongst officials. And from time to time there was conflict with their near neighbour, Pakistan, along the borders of Kashmir, in the Rann of Kutch, and, most serious, at the time of the independence of Bangladesh in 1971. The difference now was that India was free from interference by powerful foreign states like Britain and responsible for taking its own decisions in the world. Though the sub-continent's problems may not have been solved, there was an optimistic feeling that the Indian leadership could handle the problems themselves.

Bibliography
International Affairs 1939–79, R.N. Rundle
Europe & the Modern World 1870–1970 J. & G. Stokes
Asia and Australasia, J.K.G. Taylor
India, Taya Zinkin

3.2 Examiner's comments

This piece of work starts well. It discusses the origin of the problems in the first paragraph, but seems to be going off at a tangent in the last line – the question is not about the slow progress towards independence, nor Britain's reluctance to grant it. But the work gets back on course immediately; the problems arising from independence are tackled, and the last paragraph makes a good assessment in answer to the question posed 'How far?' The writing has a mature style and a good vocabulary, and the work concludes with a brief, but useful bibliography, the last book showing some imagination.

The work is probably not much over 400 words, and as such seems rather short for the requirements of most examining Groups. There were in fact other problems that could have been tackled here eg the caste system. But nevertheless the work deserves to gain a mark at a high level.

UNIT 4 STRESEMANN

Assessment objective 3: empathy.

> Write an obituary for Gustav Stresemann, the German Foreign Minister, as might have appeared in a British newspaper a day or so after Stresemann's death in October 1929. The author would be the newspaper's German correspondent.

4.1 Student's answer

> Stresemann will always be remembered for the way in which he handled Germany's economy at the time of the great inflation, and for his expertise in dealing with the crisis brought about by the French invasion of the Ruhr. In 1926 he won the Nobel Peace Prize with Briand, the French Foreign Minister, largely because of his efforts to ensure that war would never again occur. Stresemann was a great statesman and a shrewd politician; he made Germany respectable by joining the League of Nations in 1926, and he was always willing to make treaties with other countries. He paid off a lot of the reparations and managed to secure substantial reductions on what was still owing. So it could be said that he depended too much on foreign aid, and that he was unable to control extremist parties of both right and left in Germany.
>
> He has left firm foundations upon which future generations of German politicians can build. A large turn-out is expected for his funeral as he was such a popular leader. Many shops and businesses here have closed out of respect, as he was much loved here in Germany, and he will be greatly missed both here and abroad. Tributes from foreign leaders have already started to arrive; his death is a great loss to Germany's economic recovery and to world politics.
>
> The majority of British and French people will be sorry to see him go. I think that most of them recognised that Stresemann wanted peace and stability to come to Europe. There will be some people, however, who will not be sorry, people with old anger for Germany and her past misdeeds.

4.2 Examiner's comments

This exercise is a form of role-play and is not a suitable coursework assignment.

The candidate will have to look at differing views on Stresemann if he wants to achieve Level 3 (differentiated empathy, showing that not all people in the past thought the same about Stresemann's death) but unfortunately this does not appear until the last paragraph, and then has no historical substance to support the opinion, except a vague hint about the First World War. The historical content overall is thin, and this is not surprising, considering that the length of the answer is only about 250 words.

Even so there are some worthwhile things about this piece of work. Its vocabulary is good; it makes a number of useful judgements about Stresemann's work, and it does not lapse into narrative. In the second paragraph there is an interesting attempt to produce contemporary authenticity in the way the student handles the funeral. The quality of the assignment, however, could be much improved with greater depth, close attention to expanding the last paragraph, an attempt to produce differentiated empathy, and a bibliography at the end.

UNIT 5 — MUSSOLINI

Assessment objective 3: empathy.

Explain your reaction as an Italian if you have just heard that:
a) The Fascists have been successful in the 1924 elections.
b) The Lateran treaties have just been signed.
c) Your son wants to joint the Balilla.
d) Mussolini has announced the completion of the conquest of Abyssinia.
e) Italy has entered the Second World War.
(Word limit: 1,000)

5.1 Student's answer

a) The Fascists and Mussolini have just won most of the seats in parliament; they have won 374 seats out of the 535 available. I am very relieved and happy about this, for at last we have a leader in our country who has done something positive with his power. Before the Fascists took over Italy was a depressed and desperate nation: now, today, it is more prosperous and has a future we would never have expected a few years ago when we were ruled by the socialists. Already in Italy Mussolini has carried out a great number of improvements, including new roads, better transport and major public works. Also, most importantly, in the short time he has been Prime Minister, Italy has had a major success in Europe. When one of our generals was brutally murdered in Greece in 1923 we occupied the Greek island of Corfu for one month, before the Greeks gave in to our demands for a heavy indemnity and an unreserved apology. This great victory has gained us deserved respect in Europe: today there has been another great victory for Italy, Mussolini has taken control of our parliament, and this can only mean more glory, honour and respect for our country.

b) I have never questioned the skills or integrity of Mussolini or his government, and now I am even more convinced of the benefits of fascist rule and the greatness of the Duce. At last the split has been healed between the two most important things in my life — my country and my religion. The Lateran treaties have just been signed by Mussolini and the Pope. At last the Pope is recognising Italy as a nation and is himself recognised as an independent sovereign ruler. What pleases me most is that Catholicism is to be made the official state religion and it is to be taught once more throughout all Italy's schools after a lapse of nearly sixty years. My son will be able to grow up in a healthy religious atmosphere strengthened by the discipline of Fascism. The Catholic Action group will be able to continue its fine work, and will now be able to operate on a wider scale. I always said that this Mussolini was a skilled leader, and now he has proved himself. He has succeeded where many past leaders have failed before in healing the wound that has weakened our country for over sixty years since the Risorgimento. At last I can hold my head high as I go to church, knowing that Mussolini approves. I can also take part in politics, knowing that the Pope no longer objects to my doing so.

c) My son has just asked my permission to join the Balilla. I am unsure whether to agree, for if I don't he will be angry with me, and disappointed, and disgraced among his friends. His teacher questioned the class today to see whether they were in the Balilla or not, and asked those who were not when they were going to join. I know that joining is our son's way of serving our country and doing his duty to the Duce. However I have my reservations about the organisation as it trains children in warfare; they carry guns and wear uniform. I suppose my son will question my hesitation, so I must give him an answer soon. I am just worried what kind of effect membership of the organisation will have on him. I think I will give him my permission. He is just a little boy after all, who wants only to please the Party and to follow its orders. I too want to do my duty to the Party so I feel I should let him join. But it is so different in aims and methods to the organisation I was in myself — the Boy Scouts — but my son can't join that as the Fascists banned it in 1927. But I suppose my son only wants to follow the original aims of the Balilla — to defend Italy against our enemies.

d) Our leader has always, from the very beginning, promised us glory and land and an Empire. Today, in May 1936, he has succeeded in conquering our first step to the new Roman Empire. Our troops in Abyssinia have just captured the capital, Addis Ababa. We have won, and we are victorious even in the face of the sanctions imposed by the League of Nations. They thought that by cutting off our supplies they would prevent us conquering the country that brought us disgrace at Adowa in 1896. No. We overcame the sanctions, and with our Duce at our head we have been victorious, and our colony of East Africa is complete.

I am a very proud man today. I am proud to be an Italian and to be living in Italy at this time, and proud to have such a great and strong leader as Mussolini. There have been many changes in our country since the war. We were desperate and poor, and now Mussolini has given us wealth, dignity, pride and a bright and hopeful future.

e) It is June 1940 and we are now entering the war on behalf of Germany, and we shall be fighting Britain and France. It is a turn around from the first world war when we were on the British and French side, but we got nothing from that victory. Hitler, as the whole world knows, is going to win this war. Already he has gained much land, and it is a shrewd and intelligent move our leader is making. He knows that this time, apart from being on the winning side, we shall receive compensation and reward from our allies. My son is joining up, and I am a little concerned about this. I don't want him to go off to fight, but I know it is his duty as an Italian. He seems so enthusiastic about the war, as do all his young friends. However, after the Munich conference in 1938 I thought that Il Duce had secured peace for us as well as Europe. He said 'We have saved Europe', but now we are at war with Europe. My only hope is that the tide of fortune will not turn against Hitler, and therefore against us too, for we cannot stand another humiliation and defeat.

5.2 Examiner's comments

This is a more detailed exercise of the role-play type. The student uses good historical background to portray himself as a typical supporter of Mussolini, although in (a) some of Mussolini's achievements referred to may well have been after 1924. The narrative approach is again avoided, but there is a tendency for the praise to become a little repetitive (although this is how it must have been in Mussolini's time), and sometimes the historical references are a little vague and obscure.

Even so the quality is sufficiently sustained for the award of a high mark in Level 2 (stereotyped empathy), but the suggestion of uncertainty and inner conflict in the Balilla section and at the end of the final section take this into Level 3. Unswerving devotion to Mussolini is stereotyped: the student could have been more strongly Level 3 if either his own doubts about Mussolini had been more forcefully put, or if he had mentioned the misgivings of others. This Italian is a little inconsistent: he seems to be supporting all that Mussolini stands for and is, and yet regrets that his son should either join the Balilla or enrol for the war. Either the Italian would have been a good deal more critical on all counts, or else would have fully supported his son's patriotic wishes. By making the Italian inconsistent the student has reached Level 3, but he could have done it by having him more consistently pro- or anti-Mussolini, and referring to the differing opinions of the Italian's contemporaries to reach Level 3 by a different route. You will have noticed that this exercise exceeds the 1,000 word limit, but not by a very significant margin. As in the previous example, there is no bibliography to list the books consulted. But on the whole this is a well-written exercise deserving a high mark.

UNIT 6 UN TROOP INVOLVEMENT

Assessment objective 1: recall, presentation and communication.

Assignments involving pure recall will be more properly examined in the written examination (see p. 2). However, assignments are sometimes set which enable candidates to show their ability to undertake a historical enquiry and to communicate their historical knowledge and understanding of a topic in a narrative which gives a clear and accurate description of a topic. Such an assignment, according to the stated *objectives*, will require the candidate to 'recall and select knowledge relevant to the context and to deploy it in a clear and coherent form.' In such assignments, it will not be so much the *recall* which will be rewarded as the *selection* and the *clarity of presentation*. Let us take an example of this kind of coursework.

> Construct a date-list of UN troop involvement in world problems in the thirty years after 1950, illustrating your answer with a series of maps relating to this troop involvement. Write about 300 words to describe the events that took place in the *three* most important areas of their involvement.

6.1 Student's answer

1950	1950–53 UN troops in Korea
	1956 Suez Crisis, UN Emergency Force in Egypt
1960	1960–64 UN forces in Congo
	1962 Missiles Crisis, Blockade of Cuba
	1964 UN troops sent to Cyprus
	1964–75 Vietnam War, Troop intervention
	1966–70 Nigerian civil war
1970	
	1975 Civil war in Angola
1980	
	1983 Multinational force in Lebanon

UNITED NATIONS DATELINE

CHAPTER 5 UN TROOP INVOLVEMENT

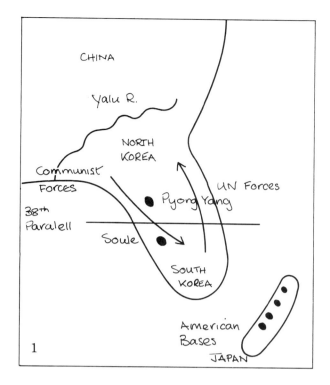

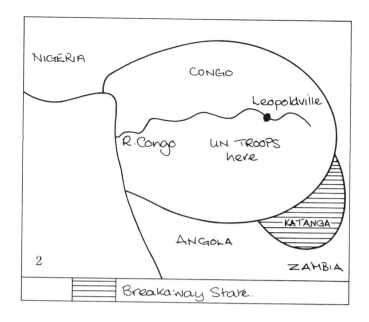

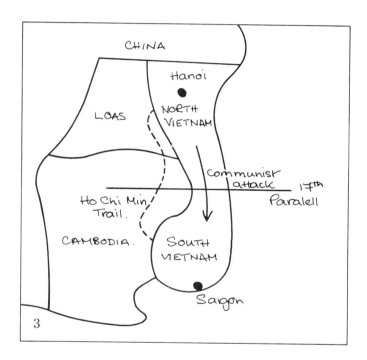

The first most important area was Korea. Here a ruthless communist regime in the north decided to invade the south to overtake it in 1950, because they hated the democratic government of Syngman Rhee. Their troops advanced south, capturing the South Korean capital Seoul and pushing the weaker forces of the democratic government almost into the sea. But just in the knick of time the USA brought the matter before the Security Counsil and they agreed that United Nations armies should be sent in to help the south of the country. The armies were contributed from more than thirty countries all over the world, and they were soon successful. The south of the country was liberated, and UN forces went on to invade the north in their turn so that the attack could not be renewed when they left. Forces advanced as far as the Yalu River, but then the Chinese communists took a hand and sent large numbers of troops to help Pu Yi, their puppet ruler in the north. After three years, the troops were more or less where they started, and even today the two countries of

North and South Korea remain separated from each other.

In 1960 the Belgians withdrew from the Congo too soon, leaving them without anyone to take over, and the country dissolved into civil war after an army mutiny in which the Congoleese army demanded to be payed. The war was very confused and bloody, and the Prime Minister, Patrick Lumumba, was murdered when he fell into the hands of opossing forces. So the USA and the USSR agreed that it would be better to send UN troops to sort things out. In the meantime, the southern province of Katanga, which was rich in valuable metal ores, decided to break away from the rest of the country and to accept Belgian help to become independent of the poorer provinces. Dag Hammarskold, the Secretary of the United Nations, lost his life in an air disaster trying to mediate between the two sides. But in the end Katanga was restored to the Congo and the country was set on the road to sucess with UN help. Eventually UN troops were withdrawn in 1964.

Like Korea, Vietnam had been divided into two parts, north and south, at the end of the Second World War, with the Russians garissoning the northern part and the Americans the south. But when the Russians and the Americans withdrew, a strongly nationalist movement known as the Viet Minh was set up and eventually threw out the French at the battle of Dien-Bien-Phu in 1954. Ho Chi Minh's forces started to infilltrate the country after the agreement at Geneva that he would not do so. The Americans were naturally angry and began to send help to the democratic side at first just advisers but then afterwards troops until there was almost half a million of them. The United Nations denounced this agression, and soon troops from many parts of the world, like New Zealand and Australia, were helping with the fighting. There was the domino theory which said that if one state fell to communism, others might easily follow and so it was best to stop the rot straight away. The troops found it difficult to keep the south free because the north kept sending help to the Viet Cong along the Ho Chi Minh trail so-called after their leader. There were massacres and helicopters sprayed the paddy fields with napalm to burn the peasants crops. Heavy bombing took place of cities like Hanoi, and President Johnson threatened that he would "bomb the enemy to the conference table." The war was long and costly and it grew more unpopular amongst the countries who had to fight it. Efforts were made to Vietnamize the war, e.g. to make the Vietnamese fight it themselves, but they would not do so. In the end UN troops had to be withdrawn and the country was reunited under North Vietnamese leadership.

In all these wars, the communist Eastern bloc were strongly against what the United Nations was trying to do, except in the case of the Congo, and even here the USSR thought it was a plot to keep Belgian mining corporations in business and to prolong imperialist control. So the Russians always exersised their veto in the Security Counsil and never agreed that the war was a good thing. The United Nations had become a battleground for their rivalries, and instead of being the impartial international body that it was designed for, it was no more than a vehicle for their national hopes and aspirations. But there was not doubt as Mr. Churchill had said many years earlier that "jar jar was better than war war."

P.S. I know this is too long but I hope it doesn't matter.

Bibliography
Catchpole, B. A Map History of the Modern World
Chadwick, John International Organizations
Gibbons & Morican The League of Nations and UNO
Rayner, E.G. International Affairs
Watson, J.B. Empire to Commonwealth, 1919-70

6.2 Examiner's comments

The student's UN date-line soon lost sight of the question's requirement. It is supposed to deal with *UN troop involvement*, yet four of the crises mentioned here – the Missiles, Vietnam, Nigeria and Angola – did not involve UN troops at all. The representation of an involvement extending for more than a single year (which occurs in four cases) would have been better done by extended blocks, rather than for example by putting the eleven chosen years for Vietnam against the date '1964'. The dates themselves need checking: when did the Vietnam War actually begin, and is '1966' the correct date for the start of the Nigerian civil war?

Chapter 3 gives useful advice on the presentation of maps, and you ought to consult it in order to improve your work. Map 1 contains no scale nor north-marker. The labellings for the arrows and the line which bisects Korea are not easy to locate, and the arrows themselves provide only the most generalized impression of troop movements. Japan is not drawn to the same scale, and is much smaller and closer to Korea than it should be. The capital of South Korea, Seoul, is incorrectly spelt, and the labels are written in longhand which detracts from the neatness. The map is diagrammatic rather than representational, and the absence of clear labelling renders it almost valueless. Another diagrammatic map is offered in Map 2. The labelling is untidy and uses *various types* of writing, lacking any consistency. This map is also inaccurate. Nigeria does not have a common frontier with the Congo, and the position of Leopoldville is confused with Stanleyville and is several hundred miles further east than it should be (though this is not easy to measure in the absence of a scale). The diagrammatic representation distorts the comparative sizes of the Congo and Katanga. The UN troops seem to be stationed mainly in Kasai province, but their precise location is hard to pinpoint and the map is generally unhelpful.

Unfortunately Map 3 does not show much improvement. Again there is no scale and no north pointer. The lettering shows *some* consistency; at least the names of the countries are in capital letters. But the arrow merely shows that the north attacked the south, and the misspelt Parallel extends too far on either side. LOAS is a careless and avoidable mistake. Cambodia and Laos ought to have been more accurately represented: Cambodia is not in fact twice as large as Laos, as it seems to be here. However, the cities of Hanoi and Saigon are in approximately the right places.

As for the troop movements which the maps are supposed to be about, Map 1's arrows are imprecise, Map 2's troop label is unhelpful, and Map 3 does not and cannot attempt to show any UN troop movements for the very good reason that there weren't any. Even the arrow shown might puzzle the uninformed – they might very easily presume that the labelled *communist attack* was a UN troop movement.

The text, as the student himself has noticed, is much longer than the 300 words asked for. The student note at the end merely draws attention to the error, and in no way atones for writing 700 words instead of the number requested. However, please take care to note that answers which are too short penalize themselves without the examiner having to do it: and shortness is perhaps a more serious state of affairs than a piece of work that is too long. This work will still have a good chance of being put within its correct assessment level, losing only the odd mark at the most.

The section on Korea provides a generally accurate summary, though it is arguable how far Syngman Rhee's government was democratic, and more seriously the confusion of Pu Yi with Kim Il Sung should have been avoided. The section on the Congo, however, is confused. Katanga's breakaway was one of the main causes of the civil war, and the student's phrase 'in the meantime' is loosely and misleadingly used. Similarly United Nations intervention occurred *before* Lumumba's murder and not after it as is implied here. The paragraph on Vietnam is even more inaccurate. It begins with a totally fictitious partition between the Americans and the Russians, implies United Nations involvement, and talks about the withdrawal of United Nations troops. The conclusion is more thoughtful, though is not strictly relevant to the title. In the last sentence the use of the word 'jar' instead of 'jaw', as well as sounding comic, goes some way towards making Churchill's famous remark incomprehensible. Spelling mistakes in fact are too frequent throughout the text, which should have been checked before being presented for assessment.

The bibliography suggests that this candidate has done a fair amount of research, and there are hints in the text that he has more than average ability; so it is a pity that it has been so much wasted effort, for the mark here would inevitably have to be fixed fairly low. Much of the inaccuracy looks like carelessness, for coursework assignments requiring assessment objective 1 will achieve respectable marks only where the presentation is accurate, is aimed sharply on target, and is convincing and coherent. Thus here the events required must relate to UN troop involvement, and the maps need to be carefully drawn to illustrate this. It looks as though the candidate drifted into this piece of coursework instead of planning it carefully. One of his difficulties may have been that when he came to research the subject, in fact he could find little or no UN involvement taking place in the 1970s, and fell back on examples that were close to the United Nations but not directly on target. This particular problem may however be one of the reasons why this topic was selected by your teachers and deserves to be carefully considered rather than simply avoided. Just because this is a narrative assignment, you must *not* assume that any old narrative will do. This sort of coursework is testing ability to select, present and explain *relevant* material, and this task required a specific historical skill which must not be underestimated.

UNIT 7 — THE SECOND WORLD WAR

Assessment objective 2: cause and consequence.

Why did Hitler fail to win the Second World War?
(Word limit: 1500)

7.1 Student's answer – version 1

In 1939 Hitler invaded Poland. It did not take him long to overwhelm the country by the use of Blitzkrieg methods and with the assistance of the Russians to attack the Poles in the rear. Britain and France were quite unable to give Poland any help. After the fall of Poland the Germans and French watched each other from their defensive positions, and so little happened that this part of the war became known as the 'phoney war'. But things were happening at sea and there were several 'incidents' and much submarine activity.

In April of 1940 German troops overran Denmark, but had a harder fight in Norway where resistance lasted six weeks. This was longer than France, because Hitler attacked Holland and conquered it in four days, Belgium which he captured in ten days and France which collapsed in just over five weeks. It was a mistake to let the British escape at Dunkirk, a mistake which was to cost Hitler dearly later. Hitler's attempt to invade England in September 1940 had to be called off because Hitler could not destroy the RAF. This was due in part to the switching of German air attacks from RAF airfields and radar stations to civilian targets in the big cities.

For a year Britain had no allies, other than Greece (attacked by Italy in October 1940). This was Hitler's big chance but he threw it away. Instead of concentrating on his war with Britain he decided to attack Russia. Before he could do so he had to rescue his ally Mussolini from the victorious Greeks. He therefore was three weeks later than planned in attacking Russia. Early German successes ground to a halt in the Russian winter. In December 1941 Hitler declared war on the USA even though his new ally Japan refused to declare war on Russia. Hitler's refusal to let his generals make strategic withdrawals cost him dearly in Russia in 1942 (Stalingrad) and in North Africa in 1943.

In the autumn of 1943 Hitler's useless ally Italy collapsed. The Russians recaptured vast areas of their lost territory and in 1944 the unlimited resources of the USA enabled France to be invaded. Vast supplies and millions of troops established a foothold in Europe. Caught between the Allies in the West and the Russians in the East, Germany's hope of survival disappeared, and Hitler committed suicide in his Berlin bunker.

Now compare version 1 with version 2 below. Remember to check again exactly what it is that the student is supposed to be answering.

7.2 Student's answer – version 2

Hitler's best chance of winning the Second World War was in 1940. In April and May of that year it seemed as if nothing could stop him, and when France sued for an armistice in June it left Britain to fight on alone. If he could have beaten Britain the war would have been over and Germany would have won. A number of mistakes wrecked his chances. The only way to beat Britain would have been by invasion, but German naval losses had been heavy in the Norwegian campaign even with control of the air, and the admirals did not want to attack Britain until their ships were completely safe from air attack. There might not have been any troops to defend Britain if it had not been for Dunkirk. The successful evacuation of troops from Dunkirk could have been prevented: for some obscure reason the Panzer divisions which could have forced the British to surrender halted four miles from Dunkirk. It seems that Hitler ordered the halt. Perhaps he was hoping for a compromise peace with Britain before attacking Russia, but one theory is that Goering was jealous of the Panzer success and asked Hitler to leave the British to the German air force. Goering obviously bombed the Dunkirk beaches but many bombs exploded harmlessly in the sand.

Even so the survivors of Dunkirk were in no condition to fight an invading German army even if one had managed to land. Everything therefore depended on the air battle over Britain which would decide whether the invasion could take place. The outnumbered RAF fought grimly but suffered heavy losses which it could ill afford. German attacks on RAF airfields and radar installations almost crippled British resistance. Then in September 1940 the Luftwaffe switched its attention to bombing London; the RAF was reprieved, and this reprieve came because the Germans wanted revenge for a British bombing raid on Berlin. It was a costly revenge; the RAF gained a breathing space; German air losses continued to mount and as autumn approached Hitler called off the invasion.

It could be argued that the abandonment of the invasion cost Hitler his chance of victory, but to the British, alone in their fight against the Axis powers, the prospects of survival seemed slender. German air-raids in the winter of 1940–41 caused much devastation. An intensification of air attack and the submarine blockade might have pounded or starved Britain into collapse. But he had already determined to invade Russia. If this succeeded Germany's supplies of oil and food would be assured, Britain's Middle East oil supplies would come under German threat, and if Russia was under German control Hitler could revive his plans to invade Britain without having to look over his shoulder at Eastern Europe. Hitler delayed his invasion of Russia for a vital six weeks while he secured his right flank in the Balkans. He sent troops he could ill afford to North Africa to help the Italians. He might have done better to have abandoned his plans for the invasion of Russia and concentrated all his available forces in North Africa. Nothing then could have prevented the Germans penetrating through Egypt into the Middle East and cutting Britain's oil life-line. This would have been less costly than invading Russia. After all Stalin had no plans to attack Germany, all he wanted was peace.

The invasion of Russia went ahead and although winter brought the German advance to a halt the Germans expected to renew their attack in 1942. Success was still a possibility, although Russian resistance was much tougher than expected, and German success in 1942 was by no means assured. But then in December 1941 Hitler declared war on the U.S.A. in support of his new ally Japan who carefully refrained from supporting him against Russia. Hitler may have argued that by

> pouring war materials into Britain the Americans were virtually at war anyway, but Roosevelt would have had much difficulty in bringing an isolationist America into the war had it not been for Pearl Harbor and the German declaration. It was not just American war materials that poured into Britain (and Russia). Millions of American troops crossed the Atlantic to Britain. Hitler's last chance of success was to secure victory before the Americans arrived in sufficient numbers to change the course of the war. But Hitler overruled his generals, refused to allow them to shorten their lines in Russia and to make strategic withdrawals. The huge loss of men at Stalingrad could have been avoided; after that there was no chance for Germany to recover. Stalingrad exposed Hitler's Empire to attack from the East, El Alamein exposed it to attack from the South, and with these battles all chance of a German victory in the Second World War virtually disappeared.
>
> Bibliography.
> J. Martell: The Twentieth Century World.
> C. Bayne-Jardine: World War Two.
> Purnell: Illustrated History of the Twentieth Century.

7.3 Examiner's comments

Have you decided which version, 1 or 2, is the better answer? You may think that because 2 is twice as long it must be twice as good, but you should never confuse quantity with quality. Do you think that version 1 is better because it covers the whole war while version 2 concentrates on the period 1940–42? Or perhaps 2 is better because it has a bibliography?

Version 1 is a mixture of narrative and analysis. It highlights some of Hitler's earlier missed opportunities, but it tends to lose sight of the question why Hitler failed to win. In the later stages of the essay the student seems more concerned about why Hitler *lost* the war, which is not quite the same question. The student in version 2 does not waste time on the 'phoney' war. He sees several episodes as crucial to Hitler's chances of winning and concentrates on them: the Battle of Britain and its abandonment, the decision to invade Russia rather than the Middle East, and the race against time once the Americans joined the war. These may be arguable, but they allow the student to develop what he sees as the key issues, and once the tide had turned by early 1943 the war issue is no longer *can* Hitler win, but *when* and *how* will he be defeated. As the question is concerned with Hitler's prospects of winning, the candidate thought it sensible to concentrate the essay only on those parts of the war in which Hitler had a reasonable chance of doing so. Even so a brief reference to the later stages of the war, if only to show that by then Hitler had virtually no chance of winning, would have been useful.

The student in version 1 makes a good average attempt at the question. His points emerge here and there from the rather brief survey of the war, but he is showing some analytical skill. The writer of version 2 is well above average, and if his written examination papers can measure up to this standard he should achieve Grade A. He has decided in advance on the limits of the essay, and kept within them. His arguments are carefully constructed and linked together in what is called a *web of causality*, i.e. it is not just a series of separate points, but the argument is effectively woven together and has a logical sequence. Historians may be able to quibble with some of his reasoning and may criticise his bibliography for omitting the names of the publishers and dates of publication of the books he consulted, but no-one can deny that the student has achieved a high level in assessment objective 2.

UNIT 8 ABYSSINIA

Assessment objective 3: empathy.

> It is December 1935. Senior representatives of the British and French Foreign Offices are meeting to discuss the Italian invasion of Abyssinia and to see whether their countries can agree on a common approach to the problem. Give an account of the discussion.
> (Word limit: 1000)

Two examples are given. See which one you prefer and whether you agree with the examiner's choice and the examiner's comments at the end.

8.1 Student's answer – version 1

> At the time of the Stresa Conference, Italy and Ethiopia were already in dispute about the obscure oasis of Walwal on the border of Italian Somaliland. Following a skirmish there in December 1934, Mussolini demanded that the Abyssinians handed over the oasis, and also pay compensation for the deaths of thirty Italian soldiers. The Emperor of Ethiopia, Haile Selassie, appealed to the League of Nations, but was told to negotiate directly with Italy. Mussolini began to pour large numbers of troops through the Suez Canal into East Africa, and when he had collected a quarter of a million of them he attacked Ethiopia in October 1935. In less than a week the League of Nations declared Mussolini an aggressor and ordered economic sanctions against Italy to deprive the Italian armies of supplies. But it took a month for these sanctions to take effect, and several countries including Germany, Austria and Hungary defied the League and refused to apply them. Oil, coal and steel were not included in the sanctions, although Russia and Romania were willing to include them.
>
> When the diplomats met they agreed to keep the Canal open, and to exclude oil, coal and steel from the sanctions list. They did not want to offend Mussolini for fear of driving him into an alliance with Hitler. It was agreed that Italy should be given about two thirds of Ethiopia in the hope of bringing the conflict to an end, and that Ethiopia should be compensated by being given access to the sea. Nobody liked these proposals and they were soon abandoned.
>
> Although public opinion in Britain and France was hostile to Mussolini, nothing was done to stop him. Modern weapons were used against tribesmen armed with spears, and in May 1936 Marshal Badoglio captured Addis Ababa, Ethiopia's capital. Victor Emanuel became the new Emperor of Ethiopia while Haile Selassie went into exile. While Mussolini incorporated all his East African possessions into the huge Italian colony of East Africa, the League saw little point in continuing the sanctions and these were abandoned.
>
> For the League the Abyssinian episode was disastrous; collective security had failed and sanctions had failed. Britain and France had tried to humour Mussolini and to keep his friendship against Hitler, but their mild condemnation of him and support for limited sanctions irritated him and drove him into the arms of Hitler. Mussolini was now on course for the disastrous alliance with Hitler which was to lead to the Second World War and to ensure that Mussolini's Empire was to be very short-lived.
>
> Bibliography:
> J. B. Watson: Success in Twentieth Century World Affairs, John Murray, 1984.

Now compare this with version 2.

8.2 Student's answer – version 2

> Most of the officials present took the line that nothing must be done to annoy Mussolini. It was necessary to keep the Stresa Front together; only Mussolini had been able to prevent the Germans from grabbing Austria, and the German refusal to use sanctions seemed

deliberately intended to make Mussolini grateful to Hitler. One of the younger diplomats said that the damage was already done and that if we wanted to keep Mussolini on the side of Britian and France he must be allowed to take the whole of Ethiopia and sanctions must be abandoned; he was not much taken with the compromise suggestion of letting Mussolini have most of Ethiopia – Mussolini wanted it all, and he would blame Britain and France if he got any less.

Another, while agreeing on the need to give in to Mussolini was concerned about the effect on public opinion and preferred a secret go-ahead to Mussolini, rather than the public proposal for carving Abyssinia into bits which most seemed to favour. Not everyone present agreed that Mussolini should be allowed to get away with it. A few were narked at Mussolini's violence against Ethiopia; they feared for the League of Nations and its image. They considered that if the damage was already done, Britain and France should close the Suez Canal, slap oil and coal sanctions on Italy, and slam Mussolini's aggression. At least the League might be able to keep its self-respect even if it could not save Ethiopia.

Not many supported this view, though, and in the end it was agreed to put forward the partition proposal, even though it might not please Mussolini and would certainly weaken the League. Fear of Hitler was at the back of everyone's minds, but one old diplomat who had won a decoration in the first world war said that if it was necessary to fight Hitler we ought to do so now before he became too powerful and before he joined forces with Mussolini; but everyone else was appalled, called the speaker a warmonger who ought to know better than to be so mischievous and iresponsible. Despite a few who shook their heads in disagreement, most thought it had been a very successful meeting, and that the best compromise solution had been cobbled together.

8.3 Examiner's comments

I hope you did not find it too difficult to choose the better piece of work here. Version 1 is longer, it is correctly spelt and uses very adult words and phrasing, it makes good judgments about the importance of the Abyssinian crisis, and it has a bibliography which lists only one book, but does include details of the date and publisher. Version 2 is shorter, and it contains spelling mistakes, such as 'Britain'. Version 2 also contains fewer facts and there are a number of lapses of style eg 'cobbled together', 'slam', 'narked'. But have you remembered the nature of the task set? Version 1 gives a good survey of the crisis with background, but the meeting of foreign office personnel is mentioned only briefly in the middle of the work and disappears again almost immediately. What is offered is an unfocused account, and if you look at J. B. Watson's book you will see how closely the account keeps to his text and even offers considerable sections word for word without putting them in quotation marks.

The second piece of work takes us immediately to the meeting. It has enough factual content accurately presented to put it firmly in its historical context and thus avoid Level 1 (everyday empathy). But does it get beyond a stereotyped Level 2? To do that it will need to show a variety of approaches and opinion, and surely there is enough of that to take it into Level 3? The candidate seems so determined to avoid stereotyping that he does not distinguish between the French and British diplomats, who might out of their countries' separate interests have seen the issues rather differently. He also makes his diplomats more moral in their motives than they might well have been: concern at Mussolini's outrageous conduct could well have been tempered by anxiety to please a superior, or to take advantage of the situation for one's country's benefit. There is no bibliography and its other weaknesses would already have been mentioned – even so it is a good Level 3 and should score 80% to 90% of the marks. In fact it got 17 out of 20, and would have gained more than that if it was longer and written in a less colloquial style.

How many would you give for version 1? At least it has a good deal of accurate history in it, so it goes beyond Level 1. However, its over-use of the textbook and its failure to set up the diplomatic meeting places it firmly at the bottom end of Level 2. Thus it scored only 8 out of 20. You may think this an unfair reward for its accurate history, but what historical skill is there in copying from a textbook? If you thought that the first example was a better piece of work then you ought to re-read the task and the two examples very carefully. This will help you to avoid the mistakes made by the first candidate.

UNIT 9 VIETNAM

Assessment objective 4: effective use of sources.

Study the following sources carefully and then answer the questions which follow.

Source A

You can help build a society where the demands of morality, and the needs of the spirit, can be realised in the life of the nation.

So, will you join in the battle to give every citizen the full equality which God enjoins and the law requires, whatever his belief, or race, or the colour of his skin?

Will you join in the battle to give every citizen an escape from the crushing weight of poverty?

Will you join in the battle to make it possible for all nations to live in enduring peace – as neighbours and not as mortal enemies?

Will you join in the battle to build the Great Society; to prove that our material progress is only the foundation on which we build a richer life of mind and spirit?

President Johnson on the Great Society, 1964.

Source B

The Train Robbery

A cartoon of the late 1960s, showing President Johnson in the foreground. (From *Punch*)

Source C

The Tet offensive stunned Johnson. Having swallowed most of the reports claiming that the Communists had been severely weakened, he had never imagined that they could attack the US Embassy in Saigon or assault the cities of South Vietnam. But he concealed his emotions.

Stanley Karnow, Vietnam, A History.

Source D

During the Tet offensive of 1968 we did not correctly judge the specific balance of forces between ourselves and the enemy, did not fully realise that the enemy still had considerable capabilities, and that our capabilities were limited . . . Our objectives were beyond our actual strength, founded in part on an illusion of what we hoped to do rather than could do. Thus we suffered large losses in material and manpower, especially cadres at various levels, which clearly weakened us. Thus we were not only unable to retain the gains we had made, but had to overcome many difficulties in 1969 and 1970 so that the revolution could stand firm in the storm.

Tra Van Tra, senior Communist general in South Vietnam, writing in 1982.

Source E

I am more certain than ever that the bloody experience of Vietnam is to end in stalemate.

Walter Cronkite, leading American commentator, February 1968.

Source F

Within South Vietnam, apart from probing attacks and an increase in terrorism in the exposed northern provinces, activity overall declined and military casualties were running at a reduced level towards the end of the quarter. It was reported that, after some loss of momentum earlier in the year, government efforts to improve security in the villages seemed to be making further progress, at least in the southern provinces.

Report on World Affairs, London, summer 1970.

a) Study sources A and B and explain the meaning and message of the cartoon. Is it favourable or unfriendly to President Johnson? Give reasons for your answer.

b) How far do sources B–E suggest that the Tet offensive by the Communists was a political success but a military failure?

c) Comment on the accuracy and reliability of Source D, and the historical value of Source F.

Your answers should total about 750 words.

9.1 Student's answer

a) Source A is taken from President Johnson's speech on the Great Society. In it he talks of equality, the tackling of poverty and world peace. The cartoon shows a train which is being made to go faster and faster by all kinds of people including the President. They are chopping up the carriages. The cartoon suggests that Vietnam, shown by the smoke from the train engine, is very costly in terms of resources. The US economy is belching out great amounts of smoke, and this can only be provided by chopping up the wagons labelled 'Great Society'. This means that Vietnam is so expensive that reform at home (the Great Society) has to be abandoned in order to find the resources to fight in Vietnam. The cartoon is not very friendly to Johnson, because it suggests that he has to give up all his cherished dreams of reforming society and encouraging world peace in order to fight a war in Vietnam.

b) Sources B to E suggest a political success, in that Source B is complaining about the cost of Vietnam, Source C shows Johnson's amazement at the unexpected resourcefulness and daring of the Communists, and Source E shows Walter Cronkite's conversion to the idea that this was a war the USA could not win. It is not entirely true to suggest that it was a military failure. Despite the losses and long-term weaknesses mentioned in Source D it is clear from Source C that the Tet offensive had at least initial

> success in striking at Saigon and the other South Vietnamese
> cities, even if, as suggested in source D, the military cost was
> very heavy.
> c) All communist sources should be regarded as unreliable. So source
> D should be treated as suspect, especially if it was written some
> time after the events it refers to. Source F is also suspect in
> that it shows the usual western optimism about Vietnam, even when
> Vietnam was about to fall into Communist hands. It does, however,
> provide some corroboration for the General's statement of how the
> Tet offensive weakened the communists in 1969 and 1970.

9.2 Examiner's comments

This answer is only about half the required length of 750 words, so the sections lack depth and development. In (a) there is some unnecessary description of the sources, but the explanations required are quite useful. The answer to (b) is the best part of this work and there is good, effective analysis here. But in (c) the student makes a very sweeping statement about regarding all communist sources as unreliable. The origin of any source, communist or not, needs to be looked at to determine its likely slant, and an American or Third World source is just as likely to have a particular viewpoint as a communist one. Unless confirmed by other independent or non-communist sources, the General's estimate of the cost of the Tet offensive needs to be treated with reserve, but, as the candidate points out, there is unexpected corroboration in Source F. It could be, of course, that the General is pushing up the cost of the Tet offensive in order to show how brilliant, by contrast, was the eventual communist success. But the General had less need to lie in 1982, and there is a certain ring of truth in his observations. Source F may well be an accurate reflection of the situation in Vietnam with peace talks in the offing, but it may reflect the continuous American official and Western optimism about Vietnam which continued almost until 1975. The candidate could have mentioned that the reliability of Source F, a secondary source, is questionable because of its remoteness from Vietnam (London) and its reliance on unspecified reports and sources.

The candidate shows ability and skill in the limited material offered, but the mark could have been greatly improved by a more in-depth treatment.

UNIT 10 CHINA

Assessment objective 4: effective use of sources

Read the following sources and then answer the questions which follow. Your answer should not exceed 1,000 words in total.

Source A

By the test of conception, birth, development and obedience, the Mao Tse-Tung régime is a creature of the Moscow Politburo and it is on behalf of Moscow, not of China, that it is destroying the friendship of the Chinese people towards the United States. It is vital that we move quickly, while we still have many friends not only on Taiwan but also on the mainland, and possibilities of access to them. But we must not only start fast, we must start with long vision and endurance because we cannot overnight undo what has been accomplished by the best brains and skills of the Soviet Communist Party working with substantial resources over a span of 30 years.

John Foster Dulles, May 18, 1951.

Source B

In 1950 I argued with Stalin in Moscow for two months. We argued about the Treaty of Alliance and Mutual Assistance, about the Manchurian railway, about setting up joint-stock companies and about the Sino-Soviet frontier. The Chinese attitude was like this: If we disagreed with a proposal of Stalin's, we struggled against it. But if he really insisted then we had to accept it. This was because we took into account the interests of socialism as a whole. When our revolution succeeded, Stalin said it was a fake. We did not argue with him, but as soon as we fought the war in Korea, then he decided our revolution had been a genuine one.

Mao Tse-Tung, March 1958.

Source C

As late as 1948 Stalin still advised Mao, as he had advised Chen Tu-hsiu twenty-odd years earlier, to make peace with the Kuomintang; and when he was informed of Mao's plans for an all-out offensive, he dismissed them as unrealistic and reckless. The victorious Generalissimo of the world's largest army was contemptuous of partisans, sceptical of the chances of communism in China, and distrustful of any revolution asserting itself without his control and beyond the range of his military power. He was afraid also that Mao's venture might provoke massive American intervention and bring American forces close to Russia's Far Eastern frontiers. The Chinese Communists, nevertheless, pressed home their offensives until the Kuomintang, rotten inside, collapsed.

Isaac Deutscher, Stalin, 1966.

Source D

China will not take the initiative to provoke a war with the United States. China has not sent any troops to Hawaii; it is the United States that has occupied China's territory of Taiwan province. Nevertheless, China has been making efforts in demanding, through negotiations, that the United States withdraw all its armed forces from Taiwan province and the Taiwan Straits, and she has held talks with the United States for more than ten years, first in Geneva and then in Warsaw, on this question of principle, which admits of no concession whatsoever.

The Chinese mean what they say. In other words, if any country in Asia, Africa, or elsewhere meets with aggression by the imperialists headed by the United States, the Chinese government and people definitely will give it support and help. Should such just action bring on U.S. aggression against China, we will unhesitatingly rise in resistance and fight to the end.

Chou En-lai, Chinese Prime Minister in the Peking Review, 13 May 1966.

Source E

The Chinese Communist leaders are dedicated to a financial and bellicose Marxist-Leninist-Maoist doctrine of world revolution. Last fall, Lin Piao, the Chinese Communist Minister of Defence, put forward in a long article Peking's strategy of violence for achieving Communist domination of the world.

This strategy involves the mobilisation of the underdeveloped areas of the world – which the Chinese Communists compare to the 'rural' areas – against the industrialised or 'urban' areas. It involves the relentless prosecution of what they call 'people's wars'. The final stage of all this violence is to be what they frankly describe as 'wars of annihilation' . . .

Peking has encouraged and assisted, with arms and other means, the aggressions of North Vietnamese Communists in Laos and against South Vietnam. It has publicly declared its support for so-called National Liberation forces in Thailand, and there are already terrorist attacks in remote corners of north-east Thailand.

There is talk in Peking that Malaysia is next on the list.

Dean Rusk, American Secretary of State, April 1966.

Source F

At the Twentieth Congress of the CPSU (Communist Party of the Soviet Union) you suddenly lashed out at Stalin. Stalin was a great Marxist-Leninist.

In attacking Stalin you were attacking Marxist-Leninism, the Soviet Union, Communist Parties, China, the people, and all the Marxist-Leninists of the world. At the Twenty-Second Congress you adopted an out-and-out revisionist programme, made a wild public attack upon Albania and reproached the Chinese Communist Party, so that the head of our delegation had to leave for home while the congress was only halfway through . . .

Far from publicly retracting the anti-Chinese open letter of July 1963 and the anti-Chinese report and resolution of February 1964, you have intensified your activities against China by more underhand tactics. Despite the tricks you have been playing to deceive people, you are pursuing the United States–Soviet collaboration for the domination of the world with your whole heart and soul. In mouthing a few words against United States imperialism and in making a show of supporting anti-imperialist struggles, you are conducting only minor attacks on United States' imperialism while rendering it major help.

Letter from the Central Committee of the Chinese Communist Party to the Central Committee of the Soviet Communist Party, 1966.

a) Summarise Dulles's policy and proposals as given in source A.

b) How far are Dulles's views supported or undermined by the content of Mao's speech, Source B? What light does Source C shed on this issue?

c) Does Chou En-lai's article (Source D) provide justification for the attitude of Dean Rusk (Source E)? Give reasons for your answer.

d) What can you learn from Source F about the China-Soviet split in the 1960s?

e) Comment on the reliability and value to historians of each of the sources.

10.1 Student's answer

a) J. F. Dulles, the American Secretary of State, certainly seems to have a morbid fear of China. He believes that China is the tool of Moscow and that positive action needs to be taken, and quickly. Just what that action should consist of is not absolutely clear. It seems to imply a defence of Taiwan, but also some kind of action on the Chinese mainland. He appears to be threatening China, but not with anything specific. It is a general declaration of hostility and an attempt to intimidate.

b) Dulles appears to think that China is Russia's satellite. But Mao makes it clear that in 1950, just before Dulles's speech, there were considerable differences of opinion between China and Russia, that these were sufficiently significant to cause lengthy (two months) argument, and that Mao only gave in to Stalin in order to preserve socialist solidarity. But Mao is tactfully silent on Stalin's failure to support Mao and the Chinese revolution before 1949 — something which Source C deals with. In any case both Sources B and C undermine Dulles's argument, but Dulles may have been unable to think straight because the Korean War was at its height in 1951 and McCarthy was pursuing a vendetta against alleged communists at home in the USA and Dulles did not want to be accused of being a 'fellow-traveller'.

c) Chou En-lai's article, while appearing to show China in a purely defensive light in the first paragraph, seems to be promising unlimited Chinese aid in the second paragraph to any country threatened by American imperialism. This seems to imply that all American influence is imperialist and aggressive and would entitle China to embark on 'just action'. So the tone of Chou En-lai's article is somewhat threatening and hostile and hides behind an ideological smoke-screen to justify his policy. The example of Taiwan given in the first paragraph is well-chosen to justify China's attitude and to throw the U.S.A. on the defensive, but the territories named by Rusk were carefully not referred to by Chou En-lai for fear perhaps of undermining his case. Even so it would seem that all of them would qualify for Chinese help on the grounds of American imperialist aggression. Thus Chou En-lai's article goes some way towards justifying the rather exaggerated American view of an expansionist China trying to subvert Asia, Africa and elsewhere with Marxist revolution.

d) The document reveals reasons for the split. The Chinese appear to be objecting to the Russian attack on Stalin's reputation in 1956. The Russians are accused of 'revisionism', by which is meant deviation from true Marxist-Leninism, and China is resentful at Russian criticism of Albania, now a Chinese rather than a Russian satellite. These are the serious charges. The silly charge appears to be the notion that because the Russians were attempting to reject the Cold War by entering directly into negotiations with the U.S.A. they were in fact becoming agents of American imperialism. The document also reveals the extent of the split. The tone of the letter is highly critical and hostile, as might be expected when the Chinese delegation found it necessary to abandon the Twenty-second Congress of the CPSU halfway through. And the Chinese refer to what they consider hostile: the anti-Chinese letter of 1963 and the anti-Chinese report and resolution of 1964.

e) None of these documents are very reliable. A speech by Dulles at the height of the Cold War is bound to be a distortion, and Mao Tse-tung's comments in 1958 on what happened in 1950 could be a propagandist effort in view of the already deteriorating state of

> relations between China and the USSR in 1958. Politicians are
> never very reliable sources of history, and Dean Rusk and Chou
> En-lai are both putting forward the best gloss they can on their
> own case. The extract from the Peking letter in Source E is also
> obviously one incident in the propaganda war between China and
> the USSR in the 1960s, so not much reliability can be placed upon
> it as a historical source, although the events, selectively
> chosen, did undoubtedly occur. Source C is the only secondary
> source here: all the others are primary. Historians prefer
> primary sources as evidence of Stalin's failure to back Mao
> before 1949.

10.2 Examiner's comments

In many ways this answer is quite impressive. The language is very mature, there are no problems with spelling, and there is an attempt throughout to get the best out of the sources without the introduction of too much outside knowledge. In (a) there is good analysis of Dulles's speech, and there is effective analysis and comparison in (b). Here, however, it is more likely that Dulles used the McCarthy era to bolster his anti-communist stance, rather than feeling any direct personal threat from McCarthy. The notion of Dulles as a 'fellow-traveller' might have stretched the credulity of even McCarthy's closest supporters. There is good work in (c), but some comment on the use of ideological jargon would have been useful. It was a sound idea to identify both the reasons for and the seriousness of the Sino-Soviet split in (d), but perhaps the Chinese fear of US-Soviet collusion is not quite as silly a notion as the candidate seems to think. In (e) the discussion is purely on the reliability of the sources as evidence, and the general comments on the primary sources are useful, although the implication that secondary sources are, by their very nature, unreliable is misleading and inaccurate. The major weakness of (e) is the failure to discuss the usefulness of these sources to historians. Even unreliable sources can tell historians a great deal: about contemporary attitudes and beliefs, about motivation, about prejudices, about grievances. What is omitted from such sources can be as revealing as what is included.

In general the candidate has done quite well within the constraints of the task set. It may be possible to criticise the original choice of sources (all written, with no visual material etc.), and the mixture of themes within the general theme of Chinese foreign policy, but a number of aspects of assessment objective 4 have been satisfied, and this answer would have scored quite a high mark.

UNIT 11 MUNICH

Assessment objective 4: effective use of sources.

Study the following sources and then answer the questions which follow. Your answer should not exceed 1000 words in total.

Source A (from the *Hossbach Memorandum*, as reported by Col. Hossbach, Hitler's adjutant, in November 1937 after Hitler's meeting with German generals; discovered by the Allies in Berlin in 1945).

> The *Führer* then continued:
> The question for Germany was: where could she achieve the greatest gain at the lowest cost? German policy had to reckon with two hate-inspired antagonists, Britain and France, to whom a German colossus in the centre of Europe was a thorn in the flesh . . .
> Germany's problem could only be solved by the use of force, and this was never without attendant risk . . . If the resort to force with its attendant risks is accepted as the basis of the following exposition, there remains still to be answered the questions: 'When?' and 'How?'

Source B (from Chamberlain's broadcast to the nation, September 27, 1938)

> How horrible, fantastic, incredible it is that we should be digging trenches and trying on gas-masks here because of a quarrel in a faraway country between people of whom we know nothing. It seems still more impossible that a quarrel which has already been settled in principle should be the subject of war.

I believe . . . that if only time were allowed it ought to be possible for the arrangements for transferring the territory . . . to be settled by agreement under conditions which would assure their fair treatment to the population concerned.

I shall not give up the hope of a peaceful solution, or abandon my efforts for peace, as long as any chance for peace remains. I would not hesitate to pay even a third visit to Germany if I thought it would do any good.

Source C (Chamberlain's speech on returning from Munich, October 1 1938)

My good friends, this is the second time in our history that there has come back from Germany to Downing Street peace with honour . . . I believe it is peace in our time.

Source D (Churchill's speech in Parliament, October 5 1938)

We have suffered a total and unmitigated defeat. All is over . . . I think you will find that in a period of time . . . Czechoslovakia will be engulfed in the Nazi regime. We have passed an awful milestone in our history, when the whole equilibrium of Europe has been deranged . . . And do not suppose that this is the end. This is only the beginning of the reckoning.

Source E (from a *History of Soviet Foreign Policy, 1917–45*, published in Moscow, 1969.)

The Munich plotters signed more than Czechoslovakia's death sentence. They gave Hitler an advance payment in the shape of encouraging further German aggression . . . Munich was a plot of the reactionaries . . . spearheaded against the USSR, and that was its real purpose.

Source F (Low cartoon, published in Britain, October 30, 1938); see below.

(a) What does Source A reveal of Hitler's forward planning, and his relations with his General Staff?
(b) How far do Sources B and C contradict Source A?
(c) What do Sources B, C and D reveal of the differences at the time between Neville Chamberlain and Winston Churchill?
(d) What does Source E reveal of the political differences at the time between the Soviet Union and the Western Powers?
(e) Explain the meaning of Source F. What does it reveal of British popular attitudes at the time of the Munich Conference?
(f) (i) Which of the sources are *primary documents*, and which *secondary*?
    (ii) Comment on the *reliability* of Source A.
    (iii) Comment on the usefulness of historical sources such as these in explaining the coming of the Second World War.

"EUROPE CAN LOOK FORWARD TO A CHRISTMAS OF PEACE."
— (HITLER)

CHAPTER 5 EXAMPLES OF STUDENTS' COURSEWORK

11.1 Student's Answer

(a) Source A shows that Hitler intended to have a war over Czechoslovakia at all costs. He spoke to his generals in 1937 and told them that war was necessary if Germany was to make gains of territory. It was all settled except the details of what he called the 'When?' and the 'How?' Hitler's statement that 'Germany's problem could only be solved by the use of force' shows the underlying belief of Nazis that violence was manly and strong and was likely to pay off. The statement would have been even stronger if he had said '*can* only be solved' instead of *could* only be solved.' The source also shows Hitler to have been in the habit of lecturing to his generals as though they were a class of not very bright students, which cannot have endeared him to them.

(b) In Source B, Chamberlain shows himself as very anxious for peace with Germany. He has not yet quite given up hope that he can solve the problem of Czechoslovakia by negotiation, and he says he is willing to go yet again to Germany to discuss the problem with Hitler. The Source also shows that Chamberlin is not very interested in foreign affairs, and regards Checzoslovakia as a 'faraway country' and its people as one of whom 'we know nothing.' Source C shows that Chamberlain takes a ridiculously optimistic view of the outcome of Munich when he made this speech from the balcony at Downing Street on his return to London. It certainly wasn't 'peace for our time' and it is doubtful whether it could be said to be 'peace with honour.' Both these statements in any case flatly contradict Hitler's opinion in Source A that Britain and France were 'two hate-inspired antagonists.'

(c) Chamberlain, according to Sources B and C, seems a very complacent man who is only too ready to accept Hitler's assurances without checking up on them. His belief, stressed in Source C, that there can be 'peace for our time', makes him out to be very gullible. Churchill, on the other hand, in Source D, sounds a prophetic warning about the future. With vivid imagery he says: '£1 was demanded at the pistol's point; when it was given, £2 was demanded at the pistol's point. Finally the dictator consented to take £1 17 6d.' This refers to how the Führer raised his terms after Berchtesgaden, and how after Godesberg he pretended to be reasonable, but took care that his demands should leave him much better off than before. Churchill had got Hitler sized up as a bully and a tyrant, but Chamberlain took him at his face value.

(d) The Soviet Union blamed the Western powers for the events of Munich. This source calls them 'plotters' presumably because Russia was excluded from their discussions. The author here also says that the Western powers were 'reactionaries', and that they 'spearheaded' an attack against Russia. It is not clear how the decisions taken at Munich betrayed the Soviet Union, though it is certainly true that they betrayed Czechoslavakia. The notion that Munich encouraged German aggression, however, was not one confined to the USSR.

(e) Hitler is shown in Source E dropping Czechoslovakia into a black bag labelled 'Deutschland Uber Alles'. Checkoslovakia is symbolized by a small child, who has been plucked from the big bed by Hitler. There are a number of other babies in bed, too, and the order of Hitler's later aggressions is shown by the list of names on the bed-head under the title 'Ex-British-French family.' The caption says: 'Europe can look forward to a winter of peace', which was the promise which

Hitler made at Munich. The cartoon is heavily ironic. The caption means the opposite of what it says, and Hitler, with a festive sprig of holly in his Santa Claus outfit, is putting his victims into a bag instead of taking his presents out. It shows that the cartoonist and other people at the time were not satisfied with Hitler's easy promises, but anticipated a lot of trouble later. Low foresaw the coming of the war.

(f) (i) The last two sources, Sources E and F, were written after the events they deal with and so were not contemporary documents. These two are thus secondary documents, whilst the first four, dealing with events as they happened, are primary historical sources. Even though Source A was not discovered for some time after it was produced, it was written at the time of the events it deals with and so is primary. Sources E and F are also secondary because they do not deal with the events themselves, but simply offer the writer's opinion about them. Although Source F is a cartoon it is offering an opinion as much as if it were written. F is also secondary because it appeared in a newspaper.

(ii) Source A is probably unreliable. If Hitler had said it, it would be in German, but in fact the source is written in English. This may show that it is a forgery. If it is not a forgery, someone has certainly translated the document into English, and a lot may have been lost in the translation. It is possible that the translator has deliberately changed the meaning of the document so that we shall get the wrong idea. It is also significant that there are a lot of dots signifying that words, phrases and perhaps whole sentences have been omitted from it. This is also very suggestive. It is possible to change the meaning of a document completely by leaving bits out. For instance, take the statement 'I am . . . demanding money from you . . . you will be in very serious trouble if you refuse' would be quite different if the deleted words were restored – 'I am *not* demanding money from you, *in case you think I am a blackmailer who says that* you will be in very serious trouble if you refuse.'

(iii) The coming of the Second World War is still very controversial, and documents such as these sources give us a clearer view of the causes of the war. They do not all agree, for there are many different views of what caused the war. The more documents we have, the better the picture becomes. Amongst the sources here, A and D and F pin the blame for the war firmly on Hitler, but E suggests that the Western powers were to blame, and this to some extent is confirmed by sources B and C, which suggest that Chamberlain's handling of the problem was not very good. Without the actual sources on which our history can be based, history would not be based on reality at all.

11.2 Examiner's comments

This assignment, too shows good handling of historical sources. The language is good; there are few problems with spelling, and the candidate tries to get the best out of the sources without revealing too much outside knowledge. The exercise would probably score quite a high grade.

The answer to (a) makes a valid point in saying that Nazism often seemed to appeal to violence for a solution; it is less sure, however, that Hitler planned to go to war over Czechoslovakia. He certainly is prepared to take the risk of war, but he says in the extract '*If the resort to force with its attendant risks . . .*' and this seems to indicate brinkmanship rather more than aggressive determination. The answer to (b) is good, showing a good grasp of Chamberlain's rather parochial view of British interests, and seeming to indicate some degree of naivety in accepting Hitler's assurances after Munich; the answer, however, does not say much about Source A, and mentions it only in the last sentence. The candidate should perhaps have said that Sources B and C certainly show that Chamberlain was not a 'hate-filled antagonist', but it is not clear whether Hitler knew British feelings better than Chamberlain did. In any case, of course, none of the later documents dealt specifically with France, and this part of Hitler's assertion may at least have been true. The answer to (c) shows a good grasp of the differences between Chamberlain and Churchill (showing, incidentally that the candidate has looked at the rest of Churchill's historic Commons speech of October 5 – this is the part of the answer which reveals the 'outside knowledge' referred to above). It takes perhaps a simplistic view of Source C; the Downing Street speech was given on the spur of the moment, and might not have exactly summed up Chamberlain's feelings – perhaps he felt a good deal more sceptical of the outcome of the recent conference than he admitted. The answer to (d) makes some useful points, and apart from a few spelling mistakes, the answer to (e) is excellent.

In (f) (i), the candidate is right in pointing out that Source E is secondary. It may have been composed some time before its date of publication in 1969 (and probably was), but nevertheless it is written as a comment by an observer, and does not come straight from a participant. Strictly, Source F may also be secondary; but it occurs so close to the events that it could be regarded as a primary indication of popular reactions to Munich. It is incidentally wrong to say that Sources E and F cannot be primary because they offer the writer's or the artist's opinion. It is perfectly possible for a primary document to offer an opinion; indeed, most of them do. (f) (ii) is the weak link in the whole answer. What the candidate says about the dangers of translation is of course true, even though it is somewhat exaggerated; for unless it is couched in some very exotic language it is not likely that the translation will make very much difference – certainly not in the case of a language like German. The same has to be said of editing. Such editing as there has been in Source A is likely to be in the interests of brevity, and not because the editor is aiming to deceive the candidate. The real trouble with Source A is that it is reported (it is even in reported speech, and that is why the word 'could' is used instead of the word 'can'), and reported some time after the event. There is no way of knowing that this is an accurate summary of what went on between Hitler and his generals. It is probably reasonably accurate, in that Hossbach would probably have been dismissed from being Hitler's adjutant if he was too inefficient; but on the other hand these were not *minutes*, and were not afterwards signed as a correct record of the meeting. There were also a number of years between the writing of the memorandum and its discovery, and we have to be careful it has not been tampered with in the interval. In (f) (iii) the candidate produces some quite creditable, if rather general material. The answer might have scored more highly if there had been more attention to the value of the particular sources chosen e.g. a closer analysis of Source D would have revealed that it was critical not only of Hitler, but also of Chamberlain, and that it cast light on the British political scene as well as on that of international diplomacy. However, the relationship between documents and the nature of historical controversy is well observed.

UNIT 12 THE POPULATION EXPLOSION

Assessment objective 4: effective use of sources.

Study the following extracts and tables, and then answer the questions which follow. Your answer should not exceed 1000 words in total.

Source A (from the *Universal Declaration of Human Rights*, 1948)

> Article 25 (1). Everyone has the right to a standard of living adequate for the health and well-being of himself and of his family, including, food, clothing, housing and medical care and necessary social services, and the right to security in the event of unemployment, sickness, disability, widowhood, old age or other lack of livelihood in circumstances beyond his control.

Source B (from *Commonsense about a Starving World* by Ritchie Calder, 1962)

> Every time the clock ticks, day and night, there is another mouth to be fed, 120 000 extra people per day.

Imagine a column in single file passing a distribution point, receiving a glass of milk, a loaf of bread and a portion of fish. At one person per second, it would take 34 hours, with the column stretching 30 miles. To give each a glass of milk would require 9 600 cows. To give each a loaf of bread would require the wheat of 200 acres. To give each half a pound of fish would require the day's catch of a quarter of the Fleetwood fishing fleet. At the end of 34 hours another column numbering 170 000 would be coming on behind. In that year, that single file would stretch from Britain to New Zealand; that glass of milk would mean 3 500 000 extra cows; that bread-loaf, an increased acreage as big as the Isle of Wight; that fish, 90 new fishing fleets as big as that of Fleetwood. How are we to accomplish the modern miracle of the loaves and fishes?

Table D (World Use of Land, 1962, in million hectares.)

	Total area	Arable or cropped	Permanent meadows & pasture	Forested land	Other land
Europe	493	151	85	138	119
USSR	2 240	220	267	742	1 011
Asia	2 822	426	434	514	1 448
Africa	3 059	232	597	747	1 483
Oceania	856	25	377	260	194
N & C America	2 424	258	356	741	1 069
S America	1 776	72	291	902	511
Total	13 670	1 384	2 407	4 044	5 835
per cent	–	10.1	17.6	29.6	42.7

Adapted from *Commonsense about a Starving World* by Ritchie Calder (Gollancz, 1962)

Table E (Demographic Statistics from Latin America, 1968–69)

	Total population (000s)	Population density (persons per sq. km.)	Birth rate (1965–70) (per 000 pop.)	Death rate (1967) (per 000 pop.)	Infant mortality (1967) (*)	Life expectancy at birth (yrs.)	Population increase p.a.	Gross domestic product (per head in $US)
Argentina	23 982	8.6	23	8.7	58.3	67.4	1.8	851
Bolivia	4 546	4.1	44	n.a.	n.a.	45.3	n.a.	184
Brazil	90 633	10.6	37.8	n.a.	n.a.	60.6	3.1	314
Chile	9 559	12.6	33.2	9.5	91.6	60.9	2.8	585
Columbia	21 407	18.8	44.6	9.4	78.3	58.5	3.2	336
Ecuador	5 829	20.6	44.9	10.6	87.3	57.2	3.0	286
Paraguay	2 336	5.7	44.6	4.2	36.7	59.3	2.7	257
Peru	13 171	10.2	41.8	7.6	61.9	58.0	2.2	386
Uruguay	2 854	15.3	21.3	9.5	50.0	69.2	1.7	628
Venezuela	10 401	11.4	40.9	6.6	41.4	53.7	3.7	765
UK	55 534	228.0	16.6	11.8	18.9	(male) 58.5 (female) 74.6	0.6	1 573

* No. of deaths of infants under 1 year per 000 corresponding live births.

Adapted from *Documents on World History, 2: 1919 to the Present Day* eds. John Wroughton and Denys Cook (Macmillan, 1976)

Source C (from *Peru 1965: A Guerrilla Experience* by Hector Bejar, 1965)

Malnutrition is one of the characteristics of the Peruvian population, and the consumption of calories and proteins drops from year to year. Annually the average Peruvian consumes only 17 kilograms of meat, an average which covers those millions who simply do not eat at all . . . Every ten minutes a child less than one year old dies, usually from an illness which is curable. In Peru there are more than 400 000 mentally-retarded children, a situation caused in great part by the alcoholism of parents and the poverty of home backgrounds. . . .

Half the population of Lima lives in squalid dwellings of one or two rooms, which lack both drinking water and all hygienic services. It has been calculated that three million lack medical attention and a million and a half walk barefoot. . . . Since 1963 the cost of living has risen in Lima by 78 per cent. Meanwhile the crime rate has risen between 75 and 85 per cent in the last five years.

(a) How far is Source A contradicted by Sources C, D and E in this question? How do you explain this contradiction?
(b) In what different ways do Sources A and B illustrate different kinds of concern for the *population explosion*?
(c) What is meant in Source C by the term *malnutrition*? What examples of malnutrition and its effects are given in the Source?
(d) Express the statistical information given in Source D in the form of a bar graph.
(e) How effectively do the statistics given in Source E illustrate the points made by Source C?
(f) Use the information contained in *all* the sources to construct a definition of, and comments on, the idea of a population explosion.

12.1 Student's answer

(a) Article 25 in the 'Universal Declaration of Human Rights' says that everyone has a right to health and decent standards, and even to what it calls the 'necessary social services', but Sources C, D and E clearly show that in practice they do not have this right. Source C emphasizes their squalor and their lack of proper medical treatment: Source D shows that too little of the land in South America is under crops, and Source E shows that the majority of the population is very poor, and dies young.

(b) Only one of these sources, Source B, is dealing with the population explosion; the other is talking about the human rights that are supposed to be guaranteed by the United Nations. Source B does deal with it, and emphasizes that a population explosion is usually accompanied by starvation — hence the title of the book from which the source comes. This is because the queue of newly-born people is growing so fast that those supplying it with foodstuffs and milk to drink cannot keep up with it and it goes on getting longer. It is a very serious problem, and one that the author of this source expresses dramatically.

(c) Malnutrition means not getting enough to eat, so that you are not well nourished. Source C says that the Peruvians do not consume enough calories to keep them warm, or enough proteins, such as those found in meat. The average Peruvian eats only 17 lbs. of meat a year, according to the source, and some do not eat at all. The effects of this lack of meat in the diet is that children die from incurable diseases, and many of them are mentally retarded because their parents turn to drink. The author even thinks that the crime rate has something to do with malnutrition.

(d)

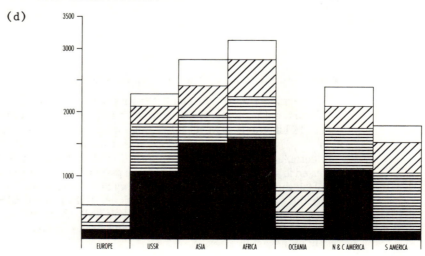

(e) Source E contains figures for Peru which bear out the points made in Source C. It shows that the birth rate is high, but that Peru has almost the heaviest infant mortality rate in the table, with nearly 62 babies in every thousand dying before they get to be a year old. People in Peru can only expect to live for 58 years when they are born, and apart from Bolivia this is the lowest life expectancy in the table. The income level, expressed as gross domestic product per head, is also low, which confirms that the people of Peru are very poor. There are no figures, however, dealing with medical services or with the incidence of crime in the table, so these cannot be confirmed.

(f) A population explosion occurs when the birth rates are very high, and a large number of babies are being born. When this increase can be contained, it is known as a 'bulge', but if it gets out of hand it called an 'explosion.' In developing countries, this high birth rate seems often to be accompanied by the high death rate, perhaps because of the poverty and lack of medical attention. Incomes are very low, and infant mortality rates are high. Life expectancy and density of population are low. If we compare the statistics for a developing country such as Peru with those for a developed country like the United Kingdom (as set out on the bottom row of figures), we can immediately see the difference. The UK is much more densely populated and has a higher income than Peru. Its birth rate and its infant mortality are much lower, and its life expectancy is much higher. This is because developed countries are richer, and so have money to spend on schools, hospitals, and other public services. Their roads are better, job prospects more promising, and living standards are better. Developing countries are often forced to concentrate on producing a single crop like coffee or groundnuts in order to service their external debt, and haven't enough left over to give their citizens a decent sort of life. Such poor countries are subject to internal weakness and strife, and natural catastrophes like floods and famines are not unusual.

12.2 Examiner's comments

This answer is quite well presented, and its standards of English and spelling, on the whole, are good. It makes quite good use of the sources provided, but tends to be rather short (about 750 words). Some of the responses are shakier than in the earlier assignments we have seen. None the less, the grade it would be awarded would probably be amongst the top three.

The answer to (a) is acceptable as far as it goes. It rather misses the point that it is because people in developing countries do *not* have the provisions mentioned that these are said to be their *rights*. Statements of rights are like blueprints for future action: there is not much point in laying stress on people's rights if they have them already. Nor does the candidate attempt the second part of the question – how do we *explain* the contradiction? If the candidate had attempted to explain it, he would have seen that the United Nations laid such stress on these rights precisely because developing cosuntries did not enjoy them. The same flaw is to be seen in the answer to (b). Sources A and B show different kinds of concerns, as the question suggests. Source A does deal with the population explosion in its own way. It makes the point that even in developing countries people have the right to health, welfare and social care, though frequently they don't enjoy it. On the other hand, the candidate shows quite a good grasp of the relevance of Source B to the problem. Quite a good grasp is shown of the Source in the answer to (c), though the candidate takes the statements made in the source rather literally. It cannot be true, as the source states, that some people in Peru do not eat *at all*: this would seem to be a figure of speech. There are other careless slips in this answer.

Calories, of course, do not exactly 'keep you warm'; they are a measure of nourishment. Later, the candidate has written 17 'lbs.' when he means 17 'kilograms;' he also says that children die from *incurable* diseases, when the source says from *curable* ones. It is also rather silly to say that children become mentally retarded when their parents turn to drink. Read the passage again in order to see exactly what the author is actually saying. Part (d) has produced a reasonable response, but there are weaknesses here, too. There are no units on the left-hand axis – it should say 'million hectares'. More seriously, there is no key given to the four different sorts of shadings on the bar chart. The shading itself could be better, and the part left white at the top is not always (especially in the case of Oceania) sufficiently clear. The small scale of the bar chart makes accurate translation of the figures quite difficult, though this attempt is quite a good one.

The quality of the answer rather improves in the last two parts. The answer to (e) is creditable, even if a little brief, and the answer to (f) is quite promising. Unfortunately it begins with some unconscious humour in the first two sentences, and this means that at the start the examiner may not take it very seriously – he will probably put a large red exclamation mark in the margin alongside 'bulge' and 'explosion.' The question, too, asks you to 'use the information contained in *all* the sources' and the answer ought to refer to them more directly than it does. But, all the same, the material which follows in the rest of the answer covers a lot of important ground. It even strays a bit beyond the bounds of the evidence in the last few lines. But (f) is, or should be, the main focus of the question, and fuller development seems quite appropriate. There are a lot of ideas here e.g. low gross domestic product meaning an insufficient capital fund out of which to finance social services, and perhaps a bit more could have been made out of them. On the whole, however, this answer finishes strongly and leaves quite a good impression.

The examples in this chapter and the model answers in Chapter 4 offer you considerable guidance in tackling your own coursework. It might be useful to *list* the main general points made in these chapters so that your work achieves the best, and avoids the worst, of the examples given here. Understand the assessment objectives, develop your skills, and coursework will be something to take in your stride. The techniques you develop here will of course also be invaluable in the *written examination*, and will help you to achieve a high grade in GCSE History.

CHAPTER 5 **PLANNING THE PROJECT**

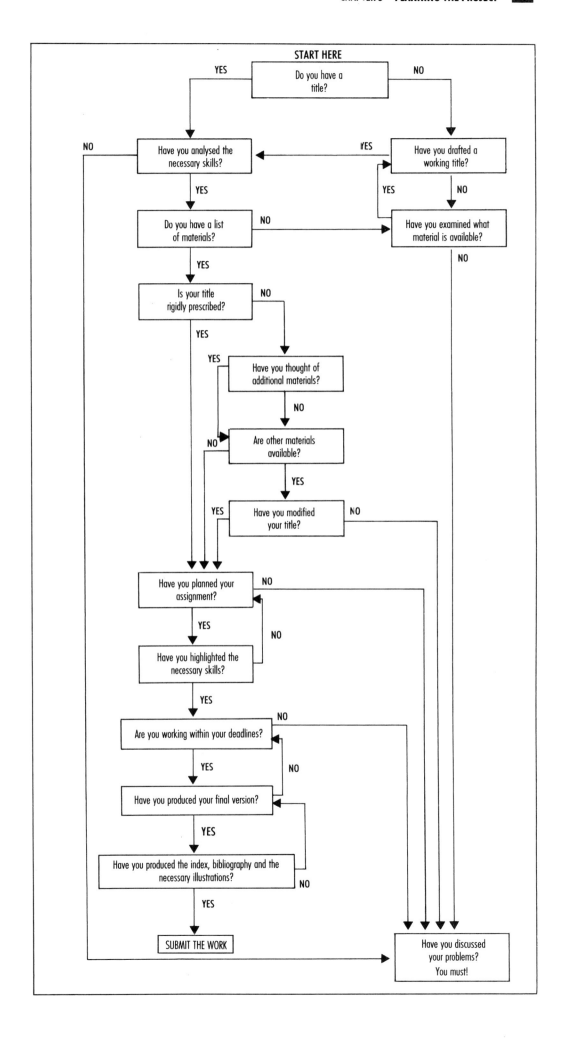